MACHINE KNITTING
The Technique of Knitweave

By the same author

Techniques in Machine Knitting
(Batsford 1983)

Kathleen Kinder

MACHINE KNITTING
The Technique of Knitweave

B T Batsford   Ltd

Photographs by Warwick Dickinson and George Kinder

© Kathleen Kinder 1987
First published 1987
Reprinted in paperback 1990

ISBN 0 7134 6568 9

Printed in Great Britain by
Courier International Ltd
Tiptree, Essex
for the publishers B.T. Batsford Ltd
4 Fitzhardinge Street, London W1H 0AH

For my mother

Acknowledgements

Grateful thanks to Jay and Vivian Davies, Warwick Dickinson, Lois Franklin Designer Knitwear, John Gibbon Knitting International, Peta Lewis Ruddington Framework Museum, Gwen Merrick, and Clare and Louise Robinson.

I am indebted to the manufacturers and importers of knitting machines and to Nobuaki Seto of Nihon Vogue, Tokyo for continued support and help.

Finally, to my husband George, not only for his photography and excellent advice, but for so patiently typing the script.

Contents

Introduction

Of all stitch pattern effects possible on the Japanese single-bed machines, knitweave has suffered real neglect. Since it presents the knitter with one of the most exciting tactile experiences, this neglect is rather puzzling.

Perhaps the renewal of interest in the technique, especially in fine, fluid knitweave as well as in textured effects, is one result of the break machine knitting has had to make with hand knitting. Knitweave can never be described as a mechanised copy of anything the modern hand knitter is doing. Neither has knitweave much in common with loom-woven cloth, though there are similarities, which are discussed in the text.

There is a keen desire to bring a distinctive view of machine knit fashion and art-craft forms to the public's notice by independent means. There is a growing confidence among machine knitters, which must be the result of years of sterling work, done in the many local education classes and the hundreds of knitting clubs and gatherings that are proliferating throughout the country. We are also seeing an upsurge in creative writing, pattern and technical literature of greatly improved quality. It is also very encouraging to note that machine knitting is being given more emphasis by the Design Establishment; but until the craft ceases to be practised as an adjunct of hand knitting, we will continue to hear the complaint that machine knitting is 'too complicated'. Effects like knitweave, fine yarn and skirt knitting will go on being neglected. New knitters need time to learn the technology and then time to make technology the servant of creativity. This is certainly the case with knitweave. Though I cannot see knitweave being given a special category in teaching syllabuses, there is growing interest in this distinctive aspect of machine knitting. However, if we do not have a repertoire of techniques and a basis of understanding, creative ideas will be stillborn.

In this book, I have tried to explain techniques that can be used by the home and craft knitter who specialises in hand finishes and fully-fashioned methods, but I have had very much in mind the approach of the cut and sew knitter whose methods must be speedy, but who is also interested in good appearance. I assume the reader is familiar with the basics of knitting and with the charting device, and that she has access to correctly sized blocks from which to develop the garment shapes. The ones I use are to be found in my *Resource Book Pattern Supplement* and in *The Machine Knitter's Book of the Ribber*, Vol. 1. Basic information on the charting device is in my *Techniques in Machine Knitting* (Batsford, 1983). I continue to present patterns in traditional format and have given notes for knitters who like to use pattern literature as a source for ideas and inspiration.

Machine knitting now has its culture and terminology for the description of techniques and the exchange of ideas. It is important that we use that lingua franca to avoid confusion, if nothing else. For the first time, I can recommend yarns in the knowledge that the same or similar are available in several countries of the English-speaking world. Japanese knitting machine technology is based on the metric system. Readers are reminded, however, that the standard tension swatch of 10cm is equal to 4in. When a patterning system is outside the scope of the charting device, I employ a household calculator, and, where applicable, the Magic Formula (*see Chapter 9*). The standard tension swatch of stitches and rows per 10cm (4in) has proved its value and remains the norm.

There are, however, areas of no-man's-land where one strives to find a descriptive term for different applications for a new or established technique or effect. Seamless robe knitting and an ORR (one row repeat) pattern are two such terms.

As far as I am aware, no one has attempted a

classification of knitweave types before, and I simply had to find my own labels. I wish to stress that such terms, names and labels are descriptive only and are not meant to be authoritative in any way.

1 The technique, history and development

What is knitweave?

Knitweave is the term used by industrial and domestic knitters to describe an inlay effect, produced on the single-bed Japanese push button, punchcard and electronic machines, which creates a surface on the purl side of stocking stitch fabric similar in appearance to loom woven cloth. Though knitweave is the only stitch effect to have a yarn independent of its main structure introduced into its fabric, it is most certainly a member of the stocking stitch family and beyond a doubt it is knitting. Knitweave is dominated by its stocking stitch structure more than is any other fabric produced by a setting on the carriage. We cannot call knitweave a pattern stitch in the same way as we would call tuck, slip, Fair Isle, thread or transfer lace, because there are no special cams on the carriage which are responsible for the knitweave effect. The most we can say is that stocking stitch is knitted but the carriage is set to pattern to select the needles, while the brushes direct the weft to create the distinctive appearance. The inlay yarn alters the behaviour of the stocking stitch fabric which is produced behind it, by destroying the lateral stretch and making the fabric more like loom woven cloth widthways.

What we often do not realise is that the stretch laterally has been squeezed by the inlay yarn into the stretch vertically. The inlay yarn acts more like a strait-jacket than a true weft. The lack of lateral stretch prevents droppage, while the increased vertical stretch gives superb draping qualities, especially in ORR weaves, similar to loom woven cloth cut on the bias. We can exploit these qualities in sideways knitting particularly in fine yarns. It is important to point out that some stocking stitch fabrics drape nearly as well as knitweave, and that knitweave is not unique in this respect. We could describe knitweave as a type of stocking stitch, interlaced with an extraneous weft, with the same, but differently allocated, stretch properties as stocking stitch.

Other points

The Japanese call knitweave thread-knitting or just weave. In industry the technique is known as knitweave or inlay. Please note that some Singer-Superba machines can also do knitweave.

Has knitweave any history?

Until I began to look at knitweave more closely, I would have said that it was a completely modern phenomenon, and that the Japanese single-bed machines with their pattern selection and brush assembly units were the first to produce it. Certainly, we have no record that knitweave was done on the Victorian V-bed domestic machine. A type of knitweave was, however, worked on the eighteenth-century handframe (from the 1770s onwards) to produce twilled, brocaded effects with silk as the inlay yarn. The modern Japanese single-bed machine has, in fact, more in common with the earlier handframe than with the handframe's Victorian successor. It must be said, however, that the type of knitweave produced in the eighteenth century was a true weave-knit hybrid. Selected stitches were removed from the needles and the inlay yarn was placed between. Then the stitches were returned to the needles. The above and below loops in modern knitweave occur over the stocking stitch background, and the stitches do not form a warp.

It is interesting that the framework knitters called their machine 'the stocking loom', and its fabric 'the web'. Weaving effects have never been far away from knitting. The ancient Sanskrit word *Nahyat*, which was often used to describe the prototype textile crafts, illustrates the confusion that was there at the beginning of man's experience with interweaving, linking and looping of fibre and yarn. Certainly, once knitters began to do the colour work we call by the misnomer Fair Isle, they were dealing with floats of yarn over and under at the back of their work, which were structurally independent of the main fabric.

In the nineteenth century, woven hand knitting emerged as a technique in its own right and was a favourite with Victorian hand knitters. It was done with two or more threads. The thin thread was the main or backing yarn, while the thicker weft was worked in, above and below the stitches held on the needles, in exactly the same way as in modern machine-made knitweave. The fabric was embroidered in cross-stitch, and this knitwoven, embroidered material was often used to make waistcoats for the railway navvies. In my part of the Yorkshire Dales, there is a record of a Quaker lady teaching the navvies building the Settle to Carlisle railway how to knit. One wonders why we have heard so little of the knitted garments worn by the Victorian navvy. They sound just as interesting as the more celebrated jerseys and guernseys worn by the sailors and fishermen. Again and again, students of knitting history are coming across glaring omissions as well as gross distortions of fact; but it is this kind of anomaly which makes the study so fascinating and so compelling.

Modern British authorities on hand knitting are curiously silent on knitweave, but Mary Thomas has several interesting pages with illustrations in her *Knitting Book* (*see* Further reading). In fact these pages form a useful introduction to knitweaving by machine. I cannot better her descriptions of the weaving or inlay yarn as 'above' and 'below'. In any case, where terms are established by historical precedent they are part of our culture, and we should stay with them for continuity and to avoid confusion.

The first modern machine knitweave

Though it has always been possible to place an inlay yarn across and between the ribbed fabric of a double-bed machine, the first single-bed machines to produce what we understand as

1 Knitmaster 370 (courtesy Knitmaster)

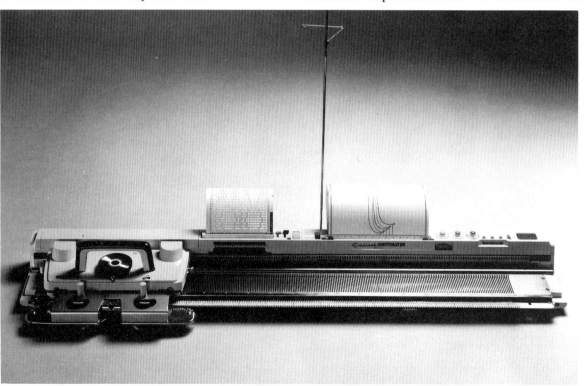

knitweave were the Japanese push-button models of the early to mid 1960s. The Knitmaster 302 had an additional knitweave accessory, which was a separate brush unit operated manually across the bed to guide the weaving yarn above and below the stitches. I remember making my first full-length knitweave coat very slowly on the 305 in 1969. This machine had detachable weaving brushes.

On the Brother 585 and 588 models the weaving brushes were built-in, and we had only to press them into place. Like the relatively unknown Toyota machine of the period, and the Brother 710 of today, these earlier Brother and Knitmaster machines had a repeat system of eight stitches, so the weaving patterns were fairly basic. I have copies of the original Brother 585 and Toyota hardback pattern books, and they are still a great source of inspiration for their imaginative interpretations of small based patterns, ORR and rolling repeat designs. A few of the Brother ones are reproduced in the 710 pattern book.

Knitweave in pattern literature

Looking through machine knitting publications from the late 1960s onwards, one can see knitweave used in terms of a 4-ply base yarn with a double knit or Aran weight as weft. (We knitters, of course, used hand knit balled yarns at this time.) Most of the yarns were smooth and untextured. Though the punchcard machines from 1971 onwards introduced us to the larger pattern repeat of 24 stitches, the yarn factor has remained unchanged until comparatively recently. Knitweave was remarkably popular during this period. Today, of course, the fine gauge Knitmaster 370, as well as the heavy gauge Knitmaster 155 and Brother 260, can do knitweave by punchcard selection. The yarn situation has not altered even with the emergence of the electronic machines with their 60 stitch repeats. In fact knitweave seems to be the least used of all the effects on the electronic machines.

When smooth yarns are used in a 4-ply base with DK to Aran as weft, the resulting fabric is moderately weighty and is best for outer wear. Smooth heavy yarns can also create a strong surface pattern similar to folk weave or coarse embroidery. This fabric is attractive in its way and is very useful for coats, skirts, jackets and furnishings, but not particularly so for sweaters and lightweight dresses. Accordingly, there are plenty of patterns to be found in 1970s issues of Jones and Brother's *Stitch in Time*, and in Knitmaster's *Modern Knitting*, which echo this theme. I can find only one dress (reproduced from *Modern Knitting*) in the *Golden Hands Book of Machine Knitting* (1973), where 2-ply is knitted as the base yarn in a very modern-looking, sideways knitwoven bodice. The machine used was the push-button Knitmaster 305. *Modern Knitting* (November 1977) featured a fluid sideways knitted outfit incorporating knitweave, designed by Esther Pearson, a finalist in the Knitmaster Design Contest. Several designers who had access to industrial yarns were doing this kind of knitweave. One of the most famous was Mary Farrin. In the Victoria and Albert Museum costume and textile collections there are examples of total knitweave. One very distinctive coat, by Kay Cosserat, is sideways knitted. Her work in total knitweave is also represented in the Crafts Council slide pack 'Knitting'.

Because nearly all the knitwoven garment patterns in magazines of the period were knitted conventionally and vertically from bottom to neck, the no-stretch situation widthways was emphasised in classic lines. Though the vertical stretch potential was there, the fabric was prevented from dropping by the horizontally placed inlay yarn. What only a few top designers had realised was that knitwoven fabric knitted sideways brought out the fluidity and the drape. In the Nihon Vogue book devoted to shadow-knitting there is a filmy, sideways knitted skirt and top incorporating knitweave, as fine and floaty as any done today. The Nihon Vogue weaving book contains some unusual and beautiful effects, and has patterns for conventional and sideways knitwoven garments. Unfortunately, both these publications are out of print.

What knitwoven fabric, knitted conventionally, did produce to perfection was the Chanel suit, and the Japanese still prefer that to any other. Perhaps the formal, trim, classic lines of the Chanel coat and skirt appeal to the situation of Japanese women; but one reason why we rarely see a more flowing look in circular skirts and tops in Japanese fashion knit magazines is that the Japanese have no coned yarn industry to support this kind of knitting. The yarns

2 Lois Franklin 'Leonardo' Italian viscose and silk
mixture with cotton (courtesy Knitting
International)

3 Lois Franklin 'Canaletto' three-piece in mohair,
wool, viscose, linen and cotton mix (courtesy
Knitting International)

appear to be getting heavier in weight. They are balled and are dual purpose for hand and machine (increasingly for the chunky machine) to provide the greatest profit. Nihon Vogue publications have reflected the change, but we are hopeful that they will be persuaded to represent mainstream machine knitting once more.

In 1976, I had three knitwoven hangings accepted on a sale-or-return basis by a famous craft gallery in the North of England. After three months, the hangings were returned because the clients thought the fabric 'very strange'.

Knitweave and the British designer

From the early 1970s, then, designers using domestic machines began to incorporate knitweave, sometimes partially, in sideways knitting, only rarely in an overall situation. Of course, conventionally knitwoven garments continued to appear alongside those in other stitch patterns such as Fair Isle, lace and tuck, which eventually pushed knitweave into eclipse, at least until comparatively recently. Unusual effects with knitweave and lace done on the Brother appeared in *Stitch in Time*, while we first saw the cut float technique in Knitmaster's *Modern Knitting* in the late 1970s.

Apart from Kay Cosserat, the one British designer who has stayed consistently with the knitweave technique since the early 1970s is Lois Franklin, once described by *Knitting International* as 'the most creative knitwear talent in the UK'. Lois Franklin has explored and perfected the techniques of sideways knitted knitweave, partial and overall, using a full range of yarns, in 'total look' dresses, as well as in coats, skirts and tops (*Figs. 2 and 3*). The style she achieves can best be described as the Laura Ashley look in knitting, in memory of a great innovator. The accent is on elegance, and the style is a perennial favourite with women who want a flowing, feminine look. If in former years that look was mainly favoured by the middle-aged and not-so-slim, there is now a clear indication that younger women want a complementary fashion to go alongside their heavy knitted tops. Moreover, this flowing style is exclusive to the machine, and many designers are now developing their own interpretations.

Apart from David Holbourne's discussion of intarsia knitweave in his *Book of Machine Knitting*, the official Design Establishment has been slow to reflect the interests of mainstream machine knitting. The 1983 Knitwear Revue exhibited only one piece of knitweave – a striking lacy evening top, sideways knitted, by Margaret Scott.

As early as 1980, Tessa Lorant had devoted a considerable part of her book *Hand and Machine Knitting* to sideways knitwoven garments, some in fine yarns. In 1983, in my *Resource Book Pattern Supplement*, I described the principles of sideways knitted skirts, and included separate patterns incorporating knitweave, using fine industrial yarns. It was as if I sensed a growing interest and felt a wind of change.

Late 1983 and early 1984 saw the publication of several books by overseas authors dealing specifically with the knitweave phenomenon. The South African authors Audrey Palmer and Rosemary Hansen are concerned with sideways knitwoven techniques for the total look as well as for separates. As a new departure, and to suit their own climate, they recommend predominantly fine yarns, down to a single strand of 2/24s or 2/30s acrylic as base. In John Allen's *Machine Knitting Book* (1985), the knitweave section is one of the most important.

Both conventional and sideways knitting present us with two separate traditions to develop and explore. I have used the standard machine in work for this book. Since knitweave can be done so easily and offers one of the richest tactile experiences of any technique, it is amazing that it has taken so long to establish its position in the popularity stakes.

2 Preliminary advice and the basic weave

Preliminary advice

Before you begin to knitweave, check that your weaving brushes are clean and that all brushes and wheels spin freely underneath the brush assembly unit of the carriage. If they do not, then unscrew them and clean away the fluff and dirt. If you knitweave according to the manual, and are using predominantly one weft yarn, then you need to keep an eye on the brake

4 Built-in weaving brushes (*top*) Brother, Knitmaster, Toyota

tension. For a DK yarn, the tension needs to be around one point looser than normal. For a 2/24 or a 2/30 base yarn, the tension needs to be two points tighter than normal. In the one yarn situation for Knitmaster machines, the weaving accessory is a good investment (for smooth yarns in particular). It speeds up the knitweave process considerably, even though it is still necessary to put out the first needle to HP to ensure a neat edge to the weave. When needles have to be held over several rows, put the first needle to C not D position.

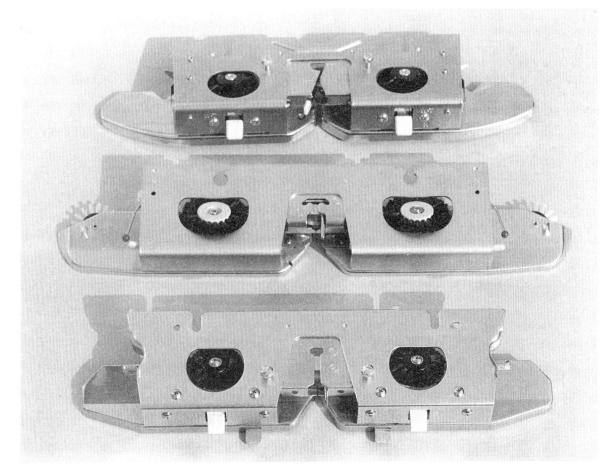

When several weaving yarns are used, have the yarns beside you on the floor, and hook the yarn inside the red knob at the beginning of each row, holding the yarn away from you so that the weaving brushes can roll it into the fabric. At the end of the row, remove the yarn while the carriage is still moving. (This applies to all machines when you knitweave according to the manual.) Bring the yarn under and around, describing an arc with your hand, before tucking the yarn inside the red knob (Knitmaster), or placing it in line with the slot on the brush assembly unit (Brother and Toyota).

On the Brother and Toyota, I usually have the weaving yarns beside me as I work. When I am using a heavily textured yarn over a full needle bed, I either lay the yarn over in two moves, or put it through the yarn brake system. Certainly, if you have several yarns to manipulate, you need to have them beside you. Let the yarn slide easily through your hand as you place it over the needles, seeing that it is laid in a slightly diagonal direction, so that it is well and truly in the hook of the last needle. Otherwise, if the yarn is too near the sinker pins, it may be out of reach of the weaving brushes, and you will have to pull back the row. In pulling back, you deal with the main yarn and the weaving yarn.

Do not work too fast, or else the stitches will drop. Use both hands, one to pull back, and the other to hold the fabric as you proceed. It is a great pity that the colour changer cannot be used to facilitate yarn changing in knitweave.

Cleaning HP needles

Before you knitweave a skirt in light-coloured yarns, push out the needles to be used, and clean them above and below with a cloth dipped in surgical spirit (untreated alcohol). Test the holding position on a swatch before you knit a skirt, to check that there are no dirty marks left on the fabric.

The use of weights

On many occasions you will find that you do not need weights. In fact, in fine knitweave, it is best to do without them. Let the fabric, as it grows, fall into your lap. In the case of a large piece, like a skirt or coat back, let the fabric drop into a large polythene bag. If you do need a little weight, especially at the beginning, then use a casting-on comb, or weave a knitting needle through the fabric (Knitmaster). Place claw weights behind the knitting; otherwise you may damage the weave.

The problem of pulled loops

Choose your weave construction and pattern with this in mind. Do not have smooth, silky, inlay yarns, which slide through the fabric, floating across a large stitch span (three or more). Knitweave can be vulnerable to pulling and plucking. However, providing the weaving yarn is not snagged, the yarn can be eased back into place, so that you cannot tell where it was pulled.

Patterns with cut floats are more of a problem. The floats can be drawn out very easily, and cannot be replaced satisfactorily. Kittens, children and cushions with cut floats do not go well together. The answer to this problem is to design a card in such a way that the cut floats do not pull out easily (*see Chapter 5*). You can also fluff the yarn with a teasel or toothbrush. Another remedy is to stitch with a sewing machine right down the centre of each solid weave, half-way between each lot of floats, but this method can spoil the look of the weave. You will need to experiment here. Practicality in design is as important as inspiration.

Casting off in knitweave: small stitch groups

Wind the weaving yarn over and under the base yarn as you knit the stitch manually before transferring it to its neighbour. Knit the two together, weaving yarn over and under, and then transfer the stitch to the adjacent needle.

The basic weave (*Fig. 5*)

In knitweave, no matter which method of laying-in is used, the weft precedes the base knitting yarn which knits the stitch. The weft is laid over the top loop of the old stitch on a selected needle, as directed by the hole or mark on the card, but it goes underneath the top loop of the old stitch on a non-selected needle (blank on the card). In the first instance, the weft looks as if it has slipped out of a trap, and in the second, it appears to be caught in place. In a repeatable, alternating pattern, the above and

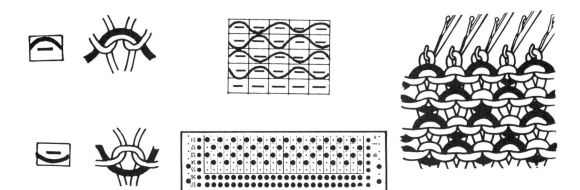

5 Japanese symbols and diagrams illustrating
Card 1 and the basic weave (courtesy Nihon Vogue)

below loops are touching. Even in a pattern like card 1 (*Fig. 7*), the weft is caught in a series of two loops, and not one as we would expect from the card. Of the two loops, the below loop is short, while the above one is dominant and appears uppermost on the surface of the fabric. It is not until we open out the fabric with our fingers that we see the shorter below-loop, hiding underneath the one above and on top.

As soon as we lock the card and create a one row repeat weave (ORR), the situation alters to a continuous repeat of the same selected and non-selected needles and their associated above and below weft loops, alternating all along the row. The fabric appearance is similar to that of twill weave done on a loom. The fact that knitweave has two main weft formations, each against a background of stocking stitch, is far more significant than any argument about whether knitweave is true knitting or not. The most important discovery is that the two types produce two different fabrics with two different tensions. The repeatable 2 stitch – 2 row pattern from the rolling card produced a bulkier fabric with a bulbous, more textured appearance. On T8 (Knitmaster 360), using a 4-ply main yarn and a DK weaving yarn, I achieved 24 stitches and 42 rows per 10cm (4in). The appearance is similar to that of folk-weave.

In the ORR pattern, the weft is more absorbed and less obtrusive. On the other hand, the fabric is flatter but more fluid. On the same tension, and with the same yarns, the swatch measured 23 stitches and 44 rows per 10cm (4in). The ORR pattern had less lateral, but more vertical stretch than the repeatable one. It is this situation, therefore, which in fine, silky-based yarns gives the greater fluidity and drape in sideways knitting.

The ORR is the pattern type which has been used for years by Lois Franklin and other designers. It is currently the subject of much experimentation in the work of Audrey Palmer and the knitweave academies she has established in South Africa. Audrey Palmer is also the first writer to explain and illustrate some of the principles of the ORR weave in sideways knitting.

The two formations and the combination

The weave with two or more repeatable rows has a hollow, diamond-shaped structure on the purl side, almost like a honeycomb. The outer edge forms a convex ridge, and the inner stitch is a purl stitch hollow. Turn over the fabric and you can still make out the weft strands around the diamond. The knit stitches are forced apart and are a little contorted. This contortion is even more pronounced in a more complex pattern shape and can indeed form an attractive pattern on the knit side. In some patterns, especially diagonals, the patterns swing, first to the left and then to the right, all the way up the fabric.

Basic stocking stitch fabric rolls inwards lengthwise, knit side outside, but knitweave fabric rolls inwards widthwise, purl side outside. There has been a fashion recently for using knitweave in straight row sections to emphasise the pleat formation in sideways knitted skirts, in conjunction with stocking stitch, lace or tuck. This fashion has been especially popular in the north of England, owing in some degree to the influence of Lois Franklin.

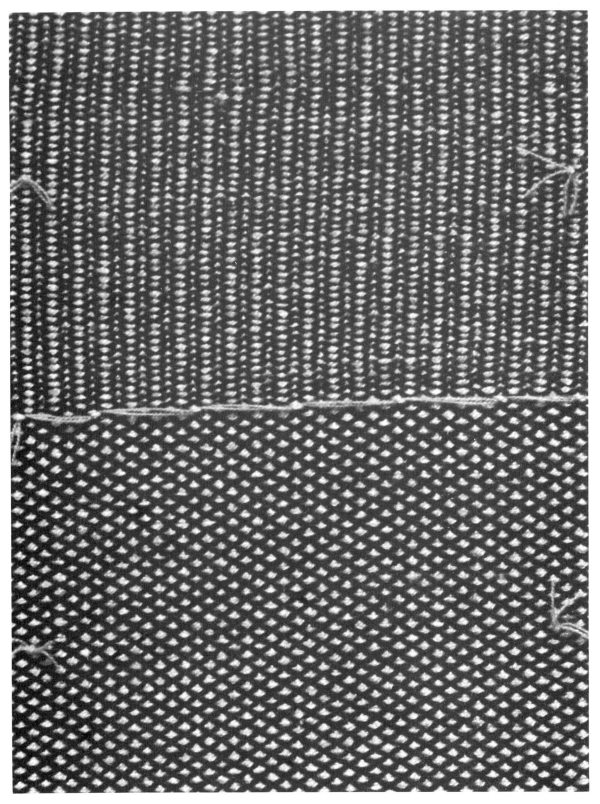

6 Swatch showing Card 1 rolling repeat and ORR
(*top*)

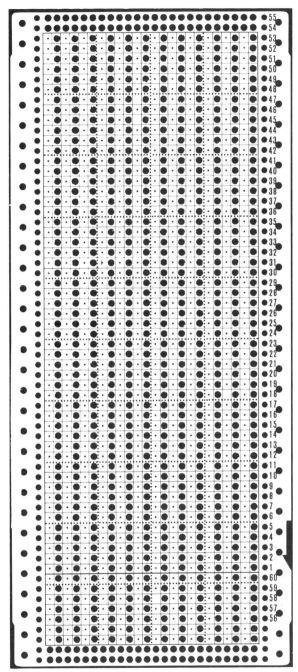

7 Card 1. ORR

Knitweave patterns are usually composed of 1, 2, or 3 weave floats spanning the stitches. Certainly, I have worked by this principle, only occasionally using floats that are longer, in the patterns I have designed for this book. The finer yarns are better with a series of 1 or 2 float

spans. Three or more float spans go better with heavier yarns. Knit the latter on a fairly tight tension, so that the floats lie close and firm and are not pulled easily. On the chunky machines, do not use float spans of more than two stitches, or else the weave will be unmanageable.

The card 1 experiment (*Fig. 6*)

Try an experiment with card 1. Use a 4-ply yarn base as I have done, and a DK yarn around T8. Let the card roll, and weave the repeatable two row pattern. Now lock the card and try the ORR pattern. Electronic knitters have their own ways of stopping the card. Knitmaster 500/560 switch on the inspection light, and Brother 910 press the CR button and select the row. On the latter machine, ignore the red error light and carry on knitting. Mk 2 knitters can use an embedded command, as I have explained in my book *Electronic Knitting*. The card will halt in each situation. It is so easy on the electronic machines to mark out a repeat that you will probably find you will do this in garment pattern knitting. Repeats should be at least 8 rows long. Punchcard knitters are advised to unlock the card after so many rows and move it manually two rows on to prevent the mechanism wearing and tearing the plastic around the one locked row. Alternatively, punch a few rows on a card off-cut, or punch out the whole pattern and set it to roll (*Fig. 7*).

If you knit 60 rows per pattern as I have done, and prepare each section for measuring, you should be able to confirm what I have discovered.

How to find stitches and rows per 10cm (4in)

The easiest way is to buy a Knitmaster green stitch gauge, and measure the swatch with that. Otherwise, use a household calculator to work out the following:

1. for stitches per 10cm (4in): divide 400 by the measurement in cm between 40 stitches;

2. for rows per 10cm: divide 600 by the measurement in cm between 60 rows.

In each answer take a decimal fraction to the nearest whole number.

Combination patterns

You can use the elongation device on your machine to produce one repeat of each pattern row. This technique makes no difference at all to the ORR pattern, but to an alternating pattern of one or more stitches, it most certainly does. The contrast is both beautiful and dramatic, especially when you stop the card altogether for a few rows and then release it again. Moreover, any differences of tension are averaged out in the combination.

Choose a diamond or chevron pattern. Let the card roll normally; then put on the elongation device. After 20 or so rows, lock the card for an ORR pattern. You have three different kinds of knitweave (*Figs. 8 and 9*). You can also contrast each one with a wedge of stocking stitch. Examine the fabric, and see how it behaves. I

like to use a simple, repeatable pattern not only with stocking stitch but with an ORR pattern in a skirt. The latter is used to knit the shaped gore or flare because it is more fluid, while the more bulbous, outward curving, alternating pattern is used on the straight row wedge to emphasise an unpressed pleat (*see Fig. 18*). The rows for each pattern are carefully counted, and punched on the same card. This procedure is very easy to mark on an electronic sheet.

Special notes

For semi-automatic machines
(8 and 12 stitch repeat)

There are still a number of Knitmaster 302/305, Brother 585/588 machines around, as well as the Brother 710. If anything can persuade knitters to use the patterning on these machines it will be the knitweave setting,

8 Diamond pattern showing elongation and card rolling and stopping

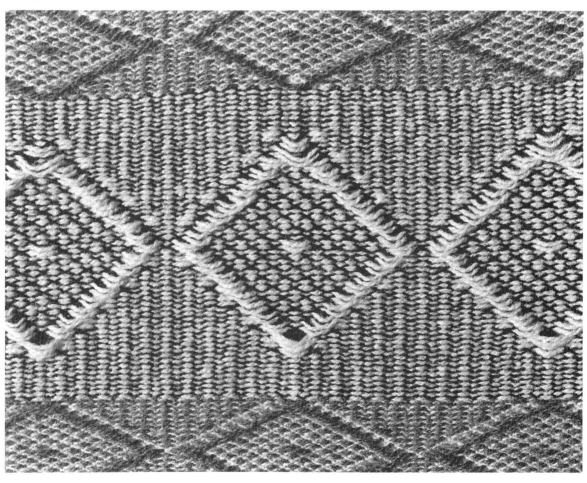

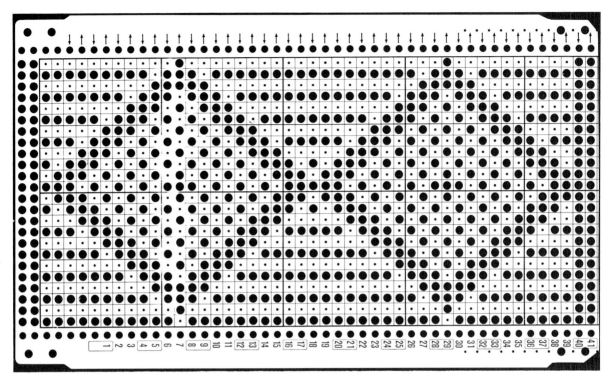

9 Card for Fig. 8

though 302/305 owners must have the weaving accessory appropriate for their machine. Check through the patterns in this book carefully. A great many can be done on the older machines. The same advice applies for the Toyota 747 machine (12 stitch repeat).

For the electronic machines

If you wish to do the patterns in this book, you are advised in the main to follow the markings on the punchcard reproductions and not use the reversal system. If you do reverse the needle selection you will not alter the pattern outline shape, but merely reverse the above and below floats. This can produce quite a significant change in some garments as far as pattern direction and texture are concerned.

Electronic knitters gain in some instances in sideways knitting when, for example, sleeves have to be carefully matched. Reversal can be achieved by using the No. 6 button in the up position (Brother), or by using the No. 1 light RHS (Knitmaster), whereas the punchcard knitter must punch the card in reverse. It is also much easier for the electronic knitter to experiment with the above and below loops to decide which direction is best for the pattern.

To centralise the patterns

Knitmaster 500/600

Place the needle one cam between the 12th and 13th needles at the left of 0. No. 1 LHS light on.

Brother 910

All buttons down will ensure the pattern is centralised, as on the punchcard machines.

The Superba/Singer machines

It should not be too difficult to alter the 24 stitch repeat patterns for the Superba/Singer electronic machines with a repeat system of 12, 20, 30 and 60 stitches. N.B.: the Singer/Juki machines are Japanese-made punchcard machines with the normal 24 stitch repeat.

3 Colour use and yarn

In recent years there has been some excellent writing from trained designers on the use of colour and on the identifications of yarn. I also discussed and described in the last chapter of *Techniques in Machine Knitting* the more common yarns on cone as used by domestic knitters.

The psychology of colour use is very interesting. We respond to colours according to our personality, and to the way the light in our environment permits us to see them, although our attitude to colour use changes with age, status and experience. In all that has been written on colour by knitters, very little has been said about:

1. The relationship of skin tones to colour, as well as that of greying hair and the ageing skin.

2. The use of colour at different stages of one's life. If the young like their coat of many colours to complement a pair of jaded jeans, then those who are older prefer the concept of elegance, represented by one colour, tinged perhaps with delicate traces of others.

3. The fact that people not only respond to but see colours differently. Response to the mixture shades is particularly interesting, where one colour strikes the eye more than another in the mix. For example, I have heard some describe a particular turquoise as more green, whereas I would have said it had more of blue in its mix.

It is a well-known fact that experts in the rag trade all too often show a complete disregard in their own dress for the teachings they give to others. Nothing is so disillusioning as the sight of a speaker, eloquent on colour, wearing a nondescript sweater from the local chain store. We should understand, however, that if colour is a game, it is also a therapy, and that even if we feel happy in only one colour, we should know why, and perhaps persuade ourselves to experiment a little beyond the known into the unknown. Moreover, we all need an awareness of colour to add to the quality of life. A surprising number of people who live in our cities see very little natural colour. They are guided in their choice by the manufactured colours of the television set.

However, when we think of knitweave, we are considering not only what colours do to each other, side by side, in horizontal bands (vertical if sideways knitted), but what the base yarn underneath does to the inlay yarn on top. Colour depth and surface contrast can be subtle, as in country tweeds, or bold, as in primitive folk weaves. In fact, knitweave presents us with the most fascinating colour experience of all, and it is one which can be available for everyone with a Japanese push-button, punchcard or electronic machine.

Sampling

Two very different aspects of machine knitting are developing among top Design Establishment knitters in the USA and in the UK, and therefore two different kinds of sampling, or trial knitting by swatch making are required. It is interesting that American knitters are involved principally in the more traditional kind of sampling.

In the USA, by using in the main smooth yarns, synthetic and natural, America's top knitters are making the most outstanding, dramatic art statements in hangings and wearable art. The work of Susanna Lewis is an excellent example of the tradition being developed by America's fibre artist knitters. They exploit large surface patterns for bold pictorial effects and appear to use mostly the Passap and electronic machines. When these fibre artists turn their talents to knitwear, they are as interested in craft as they are in fashion.

Apart from those involved in traditional Fair Isle and intarsia, top knitters in the UK do not seem to be as interested in using smooth, synthetic or natural yarns for large surface patterning. British knitters are renowned not so much for art statements as for their superb sweater craft, which they call fashion knitwear. Many of our top designers have come to machine knitting from hand knitting, and hand knitting values still dominate their thinking. This is one important reason why knitweave has been neglected: hand knitters never do it. In the UK, commercial handknit yarn interests are much more powerful than they are in the USA, and the raw material of fashion knitwear is often beautiful, heavy, highly-textured, and very expensive handknit quality yarn. These yarns do not go well with large surface patterns, and small repeats are best used to enhance the textural qualities. People could argue that, with this kind of yarn, patterning like knitweave is superfluous. There are machine knitters, both in the USA and in the UK, who are extremely versatile, and who move easily and freely from one kind of knit design to the other, though very few do knitweave. This general approach should be the objective of us all, and knitweave ought to be part of it. There is a sense too in which beautiful, highly-textured yarns can be as deadening to creativity as can an unimaginative use of punchcards.

Just as there are two main approaches to knit design as far as the yarn is concerned, so there are two kinds of sampling. In days gone by, sampling was a craft-form in its own right, as we can see from the beautiful samplers that have survived. The Victorians tried out their complicated lace patterns in one colour, usually white, and these samplers are now greatly treasured by collectors. Sampling by modern British designers is rather different, and we are concerned with that here. The traditional and modern American approach belongs to the next chapter where I discuss how to design knitweave surface patterns.

The colour game

We should allow time for preparation. Here are some suggestions.

1. If we can, we should get a representation of the colour wheel from an artists' shop. The one I use is reproduced in Fig. 10. Copy and cut it out. Colour it appropriately, paste the colour wheel on a card, and hang it beside your knitting machine.

10 The colour wheel

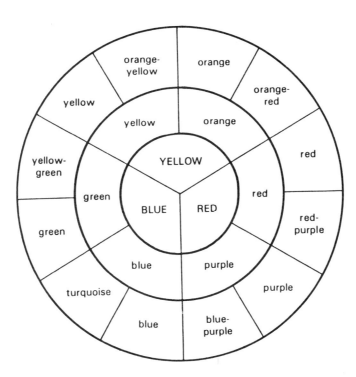

2. If you are near a shop that sells weaving supplies, or can deal with one by mail order, buy a bag or two of wool thrums (preferably DK). These thrums are usually put together professionally as far as colour combinations are concerned. Over 80 stitches you can weave between 2 to 4 rows per length. Deciding which thrums to use provides a marvellous exercise for the knitweaver.

3. Many machine knitters make a practice of collecting shade cards, just to see and feel the yarn. As a former retailer, I find it goes against the grain to tell you to acquire just for the colour experience, but many retailers do as we did and arrange the cones in the shop as the strands appear on the shade card. This underlines the initial experience, and perhaps persuades the customer to buy. Helping knitters to choose colours is one of the most rewarding and illuminating experiences of any in a yarn shop. There are people who just do not know where to begin, never mind decide which colour goes with which.

4. Go to your local decorating shop and collect colour brochures for paint ranges. These do not provide you with the tactile experience of a shade card or of a thrums collection, but the visual appeal is wonderful. If you have any wall space left, put these brochures up too. If you have no wall space then stick a selection in a scrap book to which you can add knitted swatches at your leisure, and browse over in moments of relaxation.

5. Make a point of collecting books and magazines, and of visiting exhibitions, galleries and museums where colour features largely. A very interesting place is the Colour Museum in Bradford, West Yorkshire. Jot down colour combinations that appeal to you. Above all, train your eyes to look for colour, shape and texture, and give yourself time to stop and absorb.

6. As a knitweaver, you are interested in the full range of yarn available, from very fine to chunky (*Fig. 11*). If you spin, you will be able to incorporate your own handspun yarn, again up to chunky. In recent years, a growing number of handspinners have acquired knitting machines in order to use the knitweave setting.

Most yarn shops have an oddments bin, or a 'box of delights', into which customers love to dip and rummage. Look out for oddments of

11 Yarn selection fine to chunky

2/30s acrylic, and for various fine fancies, which you can use as base yarns or as ingredients in a weave mix. There are some beautiful mohairs and chunkies on cone. There need be no problems mixing natural yarns with synthetics, providing you know how to care for the fabrics you produce. Not all smooth, high-bulked acrylics are nasty even if they are cheap; but do avoid those that are hard and stringlike, in gaudy and brash colours that set the teeth on edge, though even these can produce a pleasant surprise.

7. It doesn't take a machine knitter long to acquire cones with small amounts of yarn left from a previous exercise. Don't leave the cones rolling around in a jumbled heap. Wind off the yarn remnants and slot the ball on to a dowelling rod or a piece of card shaped for the purpose. Hand the empty cones to your dealer, or give them to the local primary school where they can be used for craft work. When you have collected a few wound balls, you will be able to arrange them to your liking on the rod. Put these beside you for inspiration and for use in sampling.

The modern British approach to sampling

From your standard pack, take card 1 and one other that has a small based pattern for knitweave. Choose one that is composed of 1, 2 and 3 stitch repeats to allow you to use heavy yarns. If you have no idea how to begin, look at your colour wheel and decide to move from one primary group and its ancillaries, say red, to another primary group and its ancillaries, say blue. Sort out your yarn into sections. Choose a neutral-based yarn to begin with. You can substitute that for another as your confidence grows and as you become interested in the change of hue it will inject into the weaving yarn above it. At this stage, don't be too concerned about the tension and the different widths. We can use ORR patterns with the thicker yarns, and repeating base patterns with finer yarns, to compensate a little. With finer yarns, we can add another to the weave mix to thicken it appropriately. Cut and sew knitters, of course, are in the best position of all when it comes to knitweaving a coat of many yarns and colours.

In your progress from one primary group to the next, especially if you use too many neutral shades, you may consider your arrangement rather dull. You have worked with a 'sludge' palette, as we call it in the North of England. Study the colour wheel again, and choose a yarn to make the colours in the sampler intensify and vibrate. Here is the arrangement for my sampler. I begin at the bottom using card 1.

The sampler: pattern and yarn analysis (Fig. 12)

1. Base yarn – Yeoman yarns Krinkle (a 2-ply acrylic-nylon gimp yarn, rather like Hobby without the knops). Colour – cinnamon.

   Weft – Patsy Kaleidoscope (4-ply). Colour – pinky white with cinnamon. Tension 2.1 on an ORR pattern.

2. Base yarn – Krinkle, as above.
   Weft – wool-silk mix 4-ply. Colour – reddish-brown.
   Tension 2.1 on a rolling pattern repeat.

I tried a mushroom pink, brushed yarn next, and rejected it after 2 rows, because the contrast it provided was unattractive.

3. Base yarn – Krinkle.
   Weft – cotton-silk mix 4-ply. Colour – grey stone and white which had an interesting deadening effect and a crisp, stringlike weave appearance. Silk is not an easy medium, but it is a very unusual and interesting one. It is best handled in a mixture yarn to begin with.
   Tension 2.1 on a rolling pattern repeat.

4. Base yarn – Knitmaster Kone 2-ply – a slightly fluffy acrylic. Colour – beige.
   Weft – Chunky gimp with pronounced loops round the finer yarn. Colour – dull pinky-brown, graduating to burnt orange.
   Tension 6 on a rolling pattern repeat.

This weave provided a dramatic textural contrast, but it was rather dense and tight. The loops tended to pierce the base fabric and stick on the sinker gate, so I had to ease them off at regular intervals. Gimp is usually composed of two yarns – an interest yarn twisted round a fine, smooth yarn.

5. Base yarn – Knitmaster Kone 2-ply, as above.
   Weft – 4-ply brushed acrylic. Colour – dusky pink.
   Tension 4 using Knitmaster Card 8 (vertical chevron), on a rolling repeat, then elongated.

12 Colour sampler

6. Base yarn – 3-ply wool. Colour – grey.
   Weft – Aran. Colour – natural cream.
   Tension 7, on an ORR pattern (2x1). A contrast was called for to lift the colour arrangement and intensify the shades.

7. Base yarn – 4-ply brushed acrylic. Colour – dusky pink.
   Weft – Chunky flecked mohair mix. Colour – fuchsia red with flecks of orange and cream.
   Tension 7, on an ORR pattern.

Two rows proved difficult, so I transferred every third stitch to its neighbour, and pushed the empty needles to NWP. (In a 2x1 pattern, take to NWP one needle from each patterning pair). The next 4 rows were easy to knit, and a very attractive, springy fabric was the result. I pushed all the needles back to WP, changed the tension to 5, and the weft to two ends of Hobby (one damson purple, one lilac), but didn't like the result.

8. Base yarn – Astrakan (bouclé poodle, 2-ply).
   Colour – grey damson mix.
   Weft – two ends of Hobby (one damson purple, one lilac).
   Tension 6, on a rolling pattern repeat.

I was delighted with this combination. Since Astrakan and Hobby are two very popular yarns, I can see this mix being used more often. The fabric is medium-weight and pleasantly springy, while the textural appeal is considerable.

9. Base yarn – Hobby (one end). Colour – damson purple.
   Weft – DK acrylic. Colour – dove grey.
   Tension 5, on an ORR pattern.

This provided a smooth and pleasing contrast with all the textural appeal and colour mix below it.

10. Base yarn – Hobby (one end). Colour – damson purple.
    Weft – Kid mohair. Colour – purple.
    Tension 10, on an ORR, lacy knitweave pattern, same as No. 7.

Hobby used as a base yarn with mohair as the weft is a sensational combination. Hobby is a 2-ply acrylic nylon, gimp yarn, with little knobs of the interest yarn appearing at regular intervals. In the UK, it has proved a best-seller for total look knitting. It is one of the most versatile of yarns. Along with other Bramwell yarns, it can be obtained in Canada, Australia and the USA, but machine knitters everywhere

can now get very similar yarns to Hobby and Astrakan. It is also good news for knitweavers that 2/24s bright acrylic is now available in every shade of the Hobby range. On the wool side, we can now match Forsell's 2/16s pure wool with a number of shades in their 4-ply Software range (wool/nylon). One strand of 2/16s makes an ideal base for knitwoven sweaters and skirts with the 4-ply as weft.

With reference to Hobby and mohair, their combined use on a lacy setting puts paid to the belief that popular hand knit mohairs cannot be used on a standard machine. I changed to stocking stitch and 3-ply Ivette (blue) as the base yarn, and used two ends of the same yarn to provide a stark contrast and a self-coloured knitweave.

11. Base – 3-ply Ivette (acrylic wool). Colour – blue.
    Weft – silky ribbon tape, heavy quality.
    Colour – sky blue.
    Tension 10, ORR lacy knitweave, as above.

This is quite beautiful. I introduced a fluffy, chunky loop weft in petrel blue, to provide a contrast, and produced the most attractive fabric on the sampler. I re-introduced the needles, set the card to roll, and did a few rows on T6, using DK acrylic in blue as the weft.

12. I returned to the very first weave pattern on the sampler. The pattern, the weft and tension are the same as on No. 1, but this time I used one end of 2/30s acrylic as the base. The colour, petrel blue, gave a pale blue cast to the weft, and destroyed its pinky hue. The fabric is medium-weight and would be ideal for sweaters.

Yarn summary guide

1. For decorative, lacy and fibre art effects.
   Base yarn – one end transparent nylon thread, or one end of 2/30s cotton, or one end overlocking thread or embroidery silk.
   Weft – your choice to suit the weave.
   Tension 1-2 (see Chapter 5).

2. For lightweight skirts, sweaters and dresses.
   Base yarn – one end 2/30s acrylic, or one end 2/24s bright acrylic, or one end Hobby, or one end 2/30s wool, or one end 2/20s brushed acrylic.
   Weft – 3- or 4-ply equivalent, wool, synthetics or mixtures.
   Tension 1-5.

3. For medium-weight jackets, tops and dresses.
Base yarn – one end 2/16s wool, 2- to 3-ply wool, synthetics or mixtures.
Weft – heavy 4-ply equivalent to fine DK.
Tension 3-6.

4. For heavyweight jackets, tops, coats and furnishings.
Base yarn – 3- to 4-ply, wool and/or synthetic fibres.
Weft – DK to chunky, including mohairs, ribbon, raffia, tape, cord and fine braid.
Tension 7-10.

NB You may have to remove needles from WP to NWP to create a more open, lacy knitweave. Knitweave does not produce as heavy a fabric as reversed Fair Isle, which can be matched reasonably well to a knitweave from the same pattern card. For a warmer top garment, therefore, use reversed Fair Isle, purl side right side, on the jacket, and knitweave on the skirt, or interline and line the knitweave as you would do a loom-woven fabric for coats. Knitweave is, of course, an excellent medium for cut and sew.

Additional notes

Balance in the fabric

If your inlay yarn is not thick or strong enough, it will be overpowered by the base yarn. You will indeed have produced a stocking stitch with a decorative inlay that does nothing to alter the stitch and row ratio. On the other hand, a too heavy inlay can make the fabric twist, contort and bell out. If it is drape you require then fine silky yarns are the ones to use.

Yarn twist

I have not mentioned cottons specially, because many have a high twist, and high twist yarns should generally be avoided. When these yarns are knitted as a base, they produce a fabric so unyielding that it would be better used as a barricade and not as a covering. High twist yarns can also destroy the finely balanced partnership between base yarn and weft by being too dominant. The cotton yarns which I enjoy using are the French 2/30s mercerised on cone which come in a superb colour range. These are soft and silky enough to be used as a base (one or two ends), or as an ingredient in a weave mix. Oiled Shetland-type yarns are good to use

as a base from handspun weft yarns, but of course the fabric must be washed to remove the oil. The general rule then, is to use soft and loosely twisted yarns for the best results.

Yarn amounts

It is very difficult indeed to give exact yarn amounts for a garment, and those that are given can only be approximate. Generally speaking, in the weight of a knitwoven garment, the base yarn accounts for between ⅔ to ¾ of the total, while the weft is around ¼ to ⅓; but these proportions do not apply when you use a fine base and a heavy weft. In that situation, the amounts could be equally divided. As far as the weft is concerned, you will use a few centimetres more than you can stretch over the WP needles, whereas you will use approximately two to three times more of the base yarn.

If you can remember, weigh the cones before you start, and make a note of the weight. Weigh them again on completion of your garment, and compare. It takes a little time to build up a table of weight references, but it is worth the effort. You will save yarn in the long run.

Sideways knitting and the weave bands (Fig. 13)

So far we have considered only what knitweave looks like in horizontal bands. What happens to the appearance in sideways knitting? This is a concern in small pattern-base knitting, as well as in large repeats. Even in small repeats, the above and below weave floats play a vital role in determining surface appearance. Take your sampler, and pick up the stitch and weave loops on one side edge, and put them back on the machine. Knitweave a band, sideways on. It might be easier to knitweave a separate band and stitch it on afterwards. If you enjoyed knitting your first sampler, try a second one, planning it first horizontally, but with one vertical band knitted afterwards.

Keeping samplers

Finally, if you are pleased with your samplers, you could turn them into mini-hangings, or mount them in your scrap book. A thing of beauty is a joy for ever, whether it is on the wall, on your back or in a scrap book. However, nothing is so depressing as swatches left lying about. Keep those you want. Amongst the

13 Sampler using thrums and illustrating sideways
knitting

rejects, select those in yarns suitable for blanket squares and give them to your local charity shop, if you don't do this kind of knitting yourself.

Generally, most people buy knitting machines to knit garments to wear, and too much swatch and sampler making can induce a sense of getting nowhere. Moreover, it implies one has unlimited time to spare, and masses of coned yarns to sample. A disciplined approach is therefore required, and an allocation of time given both to preparation and to knitting the end product. On the other hand, commercial knitters who allow no time for play are in serious danger of destroying their enjoyment and love of the craft.

4 Designing knitweave surface patterns

When knitters talk about designing their own punchcards, they usually mean Fair Isle (motifs, mostly), occasionally lace, rarely tuck, but never knitweave. Moreover, because of the current interest in ORR weaves, knitters are forgetting that knitweave is as capable of as many pattern variations as any other stitch effect. In fact, so little is known about the discipline of knitweave pattern design that I found I was venturing into virtually unexplored territory. I had to begin somewhere, so I made myself a list of all the design elements I was looking for.

1. The yarns – base and weft, smooth mostly, but sometimes textured, self-coloured, two colours or more, from 1-ply to chunky weight.

2. The visual outline of the shape – mostly geometric, but sometimes free-style (this is difficult to achieve satisfactorily).

3. The surface pattern repeat arrangements – vertical, tessellated, half-drop, half-shape (vertical and horizontal) and so on.

14 Lancashire weaving pattern

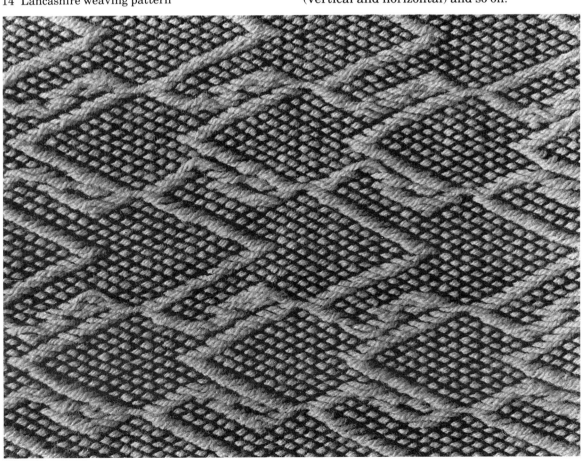

4. The repeating units of 1, 2, or 3 stitches (occasionally more).

5. Free running or rolling cards – for a representation of the design shape, or elongation, or ORR for alteration and contrast.

6. The above and below weave floats – how do you design blank and punched (marked for the electronics) cards? In what arrangement?

7. The surface ornament – in sideways as well as vertical knitting, the squat becomes long and narrow and so on.

8. The use of different weave formations to create long horizontal lines; otherwise there cannot be any.

9. The demands of total look knitting – very different from the demands of tops knitting. How do we use formal ornament in this situation? Can we mix patterns, rolling card and ORR freely?

10. The use of knitweave in fibre art projects – where do we begin? What weave patterns can we use? How much freedom have we in design execution?

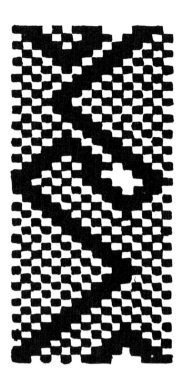

15 Electronic pattern for Fig. 14. 16sts x 42rs

Inspiration from the past

Usually when I'm looking for a directional lead, I begin by browsing through my collection of books. I have two textbooks on loom-weaving written at the turn of this century. One is for students in the West Yorkshire woollen industry, and the other for students in the Lancashire cotton industry. Even though the books were written to serve the needs of mass manufacture, the influence of William Morris and his views on re-vitalising formal surface patterns in textiles are very much in evidence.

However, the interests and tastes of people in the first twenty years of the twentieth century were very different from those of today. Because of the preponderance of brushed yarns and highly-textured knitting, we rarely see patterns with large base repeats covering the whole garment. Tapestry jacquards and intarsias are certainly in vogue at the moment, but for how long remains to be seen. With knitweave, we can reduce the size of the repeats by using fine yarns, but full-blown dolmans and batwings are perhaps the nearest garments we have to the voluminous drapes of the early

1900s. It is not surprising that we rarely stretch the patterning potential of the punchcard, let alone the electronic machine. I was, however, struck by the systematic breaking down of pattern elements and by the step by step instructions in both these old books. The information I gleaned on pattern making, I have found most useful. I do not know where I would find a modern book that would give the same kind of help. Current educational theory and practice frown on this way to creative design.

The Japanese and formal ornament

The hard-backed pattern books published by Brother, Knitmaster and Toyota demonstrate fully the skill and talent of the Japanese in the area of formal ornament with relation to all the stitch patterns possible on the Japanese machines. The Japanese may have been knitting for only just over 100 years, but they have long and ancient textile traditions in weaving and embroidery. Nihon Vogue have published a book on Japanese peasant

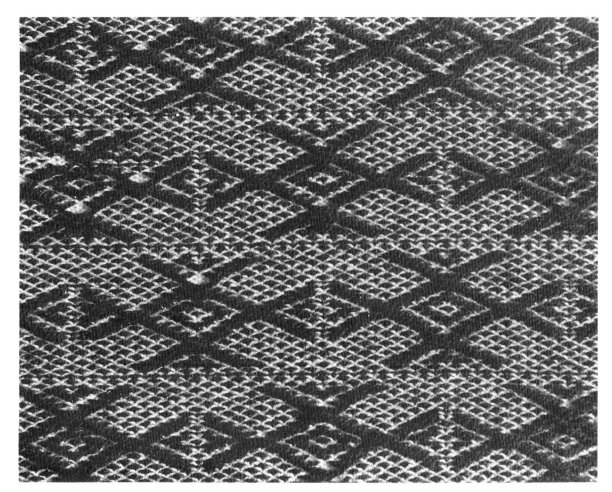

16 Japanese embroidery motif

embroidery, and I am grateful to the Silver Knitting Institute in Tokyo for sending me a copy. The embroidery is white-work, geometric and stylised, and was placed mostly on the yokes of Japanese peasant smocks. I was reminded of knitweave, and of how close it is to this old embroidery tradition. Though most of the motifs are over 30 stitch bars wide, I found a popular recurring diamond with extended arms, relatively easy to translate to a punchcard.

Large repeats need not be used all over the garment. They can be placed in areas that are most complimentary to the wearer, while the rest of the garment can be in a basic weave that is drawn from the large repeat.

For electronic machines you require only one repeat of the pattern (stitches and rows). If the position of the motif is altered, as in tessellation, then the row length of the pattern must include the two different placements of the motif. Electronic knitters can easily alter the position of patterns, but it is unlikely that they would wish to do this in garment knitting. Brother 910 knitters can take a diagonal, and with the use of the A and B setting, overlap and repeatable mirror image can form numerous geometric shapes from the one line.

Designing patterns

I have been deeply interested in pattern, colour, shape and design since my childhood. The irregular patterns and the innumerable shades of grey, tinged with rust and lichen in the dry-stone walls of the Yorkshire Dales are a continual source of wonder. Even more so are the two completely different natural colour schemes in the limestone and the millstone on

35

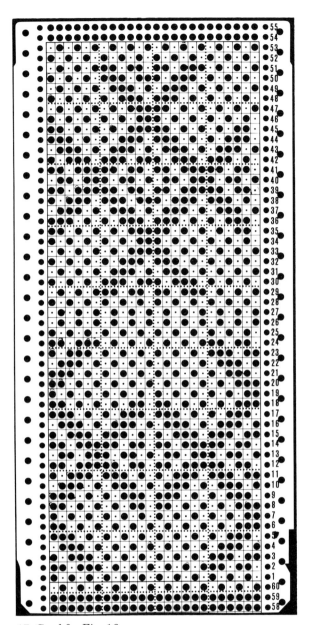

17 Card for Fig. 16

Single motifs in knitweave

We cannot get away from the fact that we are concerned with overall repeats. As you can see from the next chapter, a single motif in knitweave is in a background of stocking stitch.

18 Basic diagonal pattern for Fig. 19

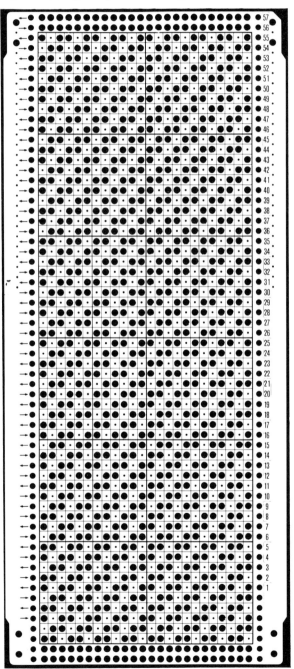

opposite sides of the Craven Fault. In the little world of the kitchen, I have been known to draw the cross-section of a cabbage before cooking the cabbage for lunch. The basis of design awareness is observation, and everyone can train this irrespective of innate ability. A careful study of Japanese knitweave patterns will pay enormous dividends. Knitweave has its own rules, which one must understand, or else the whole design practice will be beyond one's scope.

One cannot do, automatically, a single motif outline on a background of card 1, for instance. Theoretically, it is possible on the Brother 910 to do just this, by using superimposition of A over B motif, as I have shown in my book on electronic knitting, but in this direction my experiments were not entirely successful.

The main pattern shapes

There is a supplement to this chapter in which you will find a collection of my own knitweave patterns which I designed to illustrate different facets of this intriguing aspect of machine knitting.

The most common shapes are zig-zags or chevrons, horizontal and vertical. Then there are squares and diamonds, and all their derivations and variations. Diagonals look

19 Basic diagonal alternating with Card 1 ORR stripes

simple enough, but are a little difficult, because one must always be following the lines through to the other side of the punchcard; yet diagonals are the most versatile in sideways knitting. They are also versatile in sectional knitting, where one uses the same pattern on pieces of fabric tilted at different angles within the garment. The basic diagonal is a 2x1 stitch repeat (3 stitches x 3 rows). You have no need to worry about the pattern, as the diagonal forms itself with no trouble at all. It is difficult to plan a diagonal pattern based on a 24 stitch repeat, or the full pattern width of 60 stitches on the electronics. If you do not plan the repeat carefully at the side edges, the pattern will form a parallelogram.

All geometric shapes appear balanced on one apex, because long, straightforward horizontals are difficult to achieve, except by the inclusion of a few rows of an ORR pattern. Hexagons emerge as a result of elongation, used on the

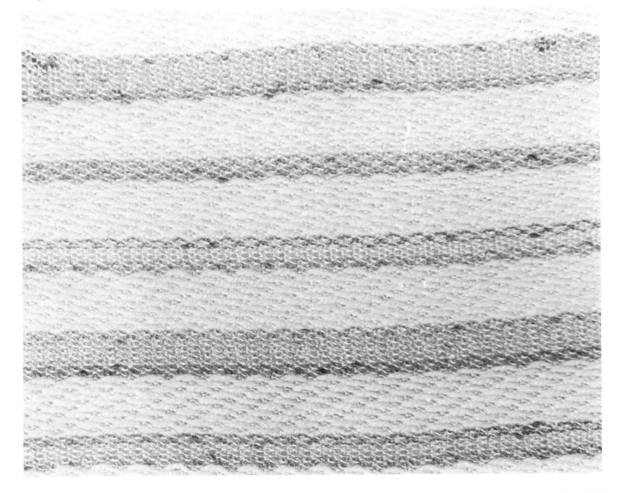

diamond shape. They have a softer outline than the square or diamond, and are very accommodating and flattering to wear as a surface pattern. These shapes – diamond, square and hexagon – develop from a series of regular steps. When we come to the oval or ogee shape, we realise that the depth of the step must vary, and that it no longer moves out in regular formation, one stitch and row at a time. The curved outline is of prime importance, and we work at the pattern freely to create the shape we want. The large oval has a widening effect and it should be used with caution by the not-so-slim.

Half shapes (vertical and horizontal) are very useful in garment design. It is flattering to have one section halved horizontally at the bottom edge, and the other section reversed, or the same way up, at the top, with a basic or ORR weave in between. A series of vertical halves, facing first one way, then the other, can be used with great effect on the yoke of a garment, and can form a striking panel in a sideways knitted top. One panel only, from the shoulder down, can be very attractive in sideways knitting.

Free-style patterns are possible, but they are best worked on a 1x1 or ORR background grid. In fact, it is best to use the two basic weaves together on the same card, designing the shapes at random in one base, and surrounding them with the other. This kind of design is very effective in sideways knitting. Indeed, it is ideally suited to the technique. More difficult are the naturalistic shapes which one has to reduce to a series of 1, 2 and 3 stitch bars, interspersed with an occasional 5 stitch bar. Then one has to consider whether the floats are directed upwards by selection, or downwards by non-selection. The most difficult of all, I find, are the shapes which involve large areas of blank, and therefore represent downward weave floats, which one cannot quite visualise in a background of alternate 1x1 or ORR pattern.

20 Flower motif (*centre*)

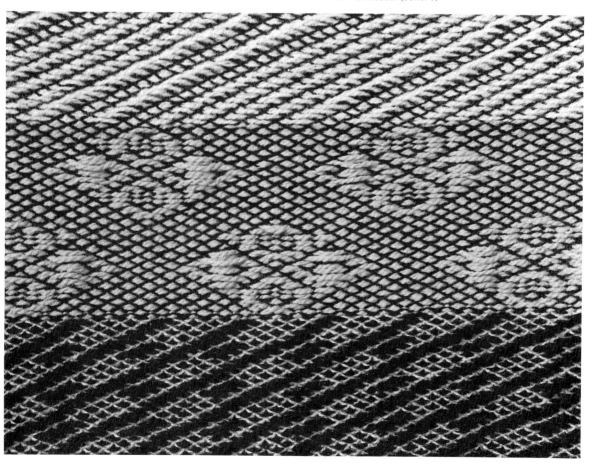

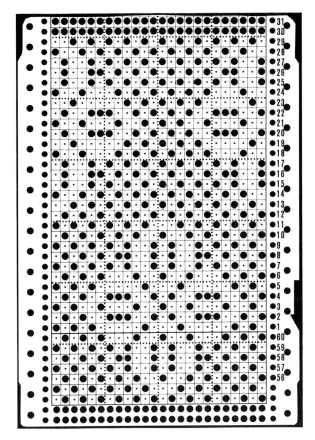

21 Card for Fig. 20 (centre)

In Fig. 21 I attempted a four-petal flower pattern, and wanted to depart from the severity of the geometric shape. Notice the two punched holes, side by side, on the outline of each of the four petals. If I had conformed to the regularity of the shape, and the rules governing the 1x1 background repeat, I would have stayed with a dissected, formalised diamond; but by leaving the holes as they are, I achieved an upward weave bar, 2 stitches long, which blurred the outline. You are at liberty to block one of the holes on each pattern, and restore the harmony. I left the design to illustrate how easy it is to get blurred and tatty-edged leaves, flowers, butterflies, animals and people if one chooses to celebrate them in knitweave. In some cases, the design is a total success and very pleasing, but one has to work at it for considerably longer than with a geometric shape (see the Paisley pattern in the garment pattern section). One gets a great sense of achievement from doing this kind of surface design.

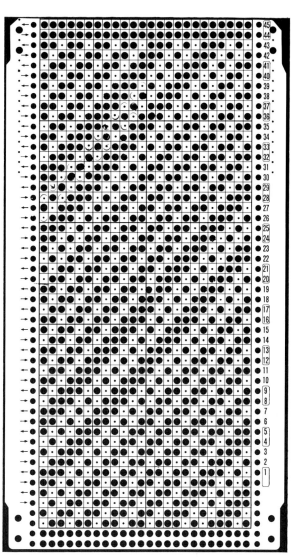

22 Card for top diagonal pattern in Fig. 20.
(See Fig. 31 for bottom pattern)

Before you make your final choice of pattern for a garment, turn the swatch over and consider whether the reverse side is as interesting as the purl side right side. Often it is, and occasionally it is even more interesting.

The placement of patterns on the card

There are three main placements of large repeat patterns.

1. The simple repeat of one or more shapes that follow on in vertical columns up the fabric. This can give a slimming effect, especially on a long jacket.

39

2. The tessellated, counterchange or brick repeat. These patterns have a harmony and a balance, and, because they are offset, give an illusion of a diagonal arrangement. They are easy on the eye, and good to wear. The flower design is an example of this type. The repeat alternates with the first shape. It is a little more difficult to plan than the first option, but if one remembers that the design half in the bottom left goes in the top right, and the one from the bottom right in the top left, there are no problems. Cover up the other parts of the card while you transfer the pattern. Some patterns, notably diamonds and hexagons, create their own counterchange patterns, identical to themselves at the side of the main vertical repeat.

23 Diamonds from Card 1

3. Occasionally, I find myself designing a half-drop pattern, where the first line of the second pattern begins about half way up the first. On the punchcard, these can appear only as a small based pattern of up to 12 stitches wide, but some diamond and hexagon patterns form their own half-drop repeat automatically. In this situation they can be 24 stitches wide.

Card locking and elongation

This is a reminder that you can vary the pattern in a very striking way by halting the card for two or more rows. In fact, in the half-drop pattern there can be interesting variations, depending on whether you halt the card on the first, last or halfway line of the first pattern, or on the first, last or halfway line of the second. I

quite often soften my pet aversion, the vertical zig-zag, by punching a straight vertical ORR pattern between the zig and the zag. Of course, the vertical zig-zag becomes a horizontal in sideways knitting.

However, the most striking effect of elongation on a pattern can be seen on designs like the diamond in an earlier chapter, and various versions of it (half and tessellated) in the supplement. Here I have contrasted the pattern repeats inside the shape with the ORR outside of it. In elongation, the ORR repeat remains the same, while the diamond and its internal pattern now become much more pronounced and three-dimensional in appearance.

Designing your own large based patterns

There are several ways to proceed towards your own original designs, both for vertical and sideways knitting. In any sampling you do, the surface design and its ultimate use will be as important as the yarn, use of colour and the shape of the garment.

1. Study the collection of knitweave cards that come with the machine to see how the designs have been developed, what float spans are used and whether they are for above or below loops, etc. If you have one of the hardback pattern books, study the knitweave section in that.

Now copy out the first few lines of a chosen pattern, either directly onto a punch or pattern card, or onto graph paper, using soft, pencilled rings. Put the original card out of sight and begin to develop your own pattern upwards and outwards from those first few lines. Do not despise this way of working. Remember that Michelangelo and Leonardo learnt their craft by copying the work of their teachers. This was the first stage in their progress towards originality.

2. If you have access to any of the stitch pattern books of Knitmaster, Brother and Toyota for the old push-button machines, learn to read the Japanese stitch symbols (*see Chapter 2*) and translate for the punchcard or electronic machines. I translated the Toyota diagonal pattern in this way. The Knitmaster 305 pattern was worked out from a photograph of the stitch found in an early copy of Modern Knitting. Because these patterns are simple 8 stitch repeats, they provide an excellent way into the design discipline.

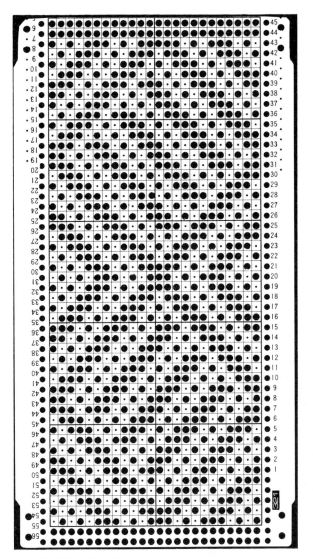

24 Card for Fig. 23

3. Another way is to take one of the border patterns in this book and develop an overall pattern from that. I leave you to find out which ones I did in this way. There can be some interesting surprises. Hexagons can develop from the slightest wave in the border pattern.

Card offcuts are very useful, and many machine knitters collect card offcuts as they collect yarn oddments. If you are nervous about punching a full-length pattern, try some borders first on your offcuts. Roll them backwards and forwards and see how they would look as overall patterns. It is, of course, very easy for owners of electronic machines: they need only one repeat anyway.

4. Look at your pattern cards for Fair Isle, tuck, slip, and punch or thread lace. Are there any you can use for knitweave? I have used cards I designed originally for Knitmaster punch lace, and am quite pleased with the knitweave result. As soon as you understand what pattern marks are responsible for which knitweave effect, you begin to see how cards for other stitch patterns would react. Moreover, you will also see how you can alter cards to make them into knitweave patterns. I have taken a basketweave pattern which I used for lined jacquard and quilting in my *Machine Knitter's Book of the Ribber* Vol. 2, and altered it for knitweave.

5. Take card 1 and punch it as an alternating pattern on a card 50 rows long (*Fig. 24*). Electronic knitters: because the pattern in the top half is different from that in the bottom, you are advised to mark 50 rows also. Now mark or

punch two diamonds, beginning with three holes or marks at the centre of the bottom line, and moving upwards and outwards, one stitch and row at a time. When you have done two diamonds, stop. Now fill them in with your own patterns by letting your pen or punch wander. Put the card on the floor and survey it from a height through half-shut eyes. Often you see how a pattern should come together when you study it with blurred vision from a distance.

6. Take a blank card, and with a soft pencil, rule lines vertically down the centre of every alternate stitch grid. In other words, you are preparing a background of the 1x1 ORR pattern. Now take your rubber and use it as a paint brush at intervals. Begin to block out an outline. Then rub out the lines inside the outline. Check that your weave floats are no more than 3 stitches wide. Since your design units are blank, the floats will be below ones. Instead of a block pattern, you could plan blisters of the 1x1 repeat pattern, set in the background of the ORR base.

25 Two free-style patterns

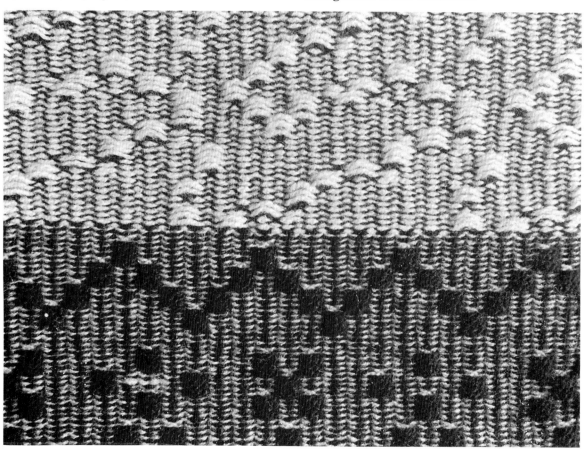

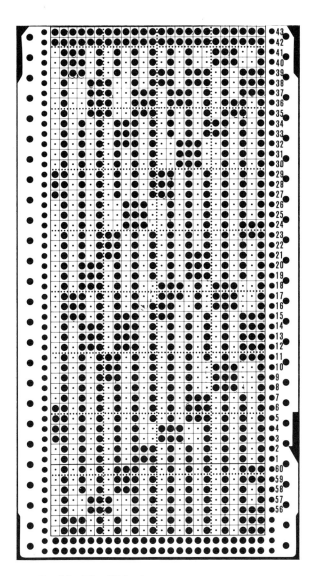

26 Card for Fig. 25 (*top*)

27 Card for Fig. 25 (*bottom*)

7. Follow the instructions for no. 6, but this time do not use your rubber. Block across at random to create a free-style design, again with weave floats no more than 3 stitches wide. This time, because you have marked and punched the design units, the floats will be above ones. Now try and combine the methods outlined in nos. 6 and 7. Leaving blanks is more difficult; but again, if you view the card from a distance, the shapes begin to appear. These designs are unusual, and contrast attractively with the more conventional knitweave patterns in a series of borders on a garment. Again you may prefer to punch on a card offcut first. These patterns respond well to colour changes, both in background and in weft inlay yarns.

When you begin to design your own patterns, without any reference to any others, you will find that you will use a combination of alternating patterns as well as those from an ORR base. You will find also that you can indeed design free-style without a strict adherence to geometry. The weave floats, above and below, will also vary in length. Remember to try to avoid floats crossing more than three stitches on a garment which is for practical use and which is going to be subjected to a lot of hard wear.

43

▲ 28 Embroidered parellelograms   ▼ 29 Diagonal pattern from a symbol chart (Toyota)

Float faults in knitweave

This problem occurs on some machines more than on others. There appears to be a mis-pattern, and the weaving yarn floats where it should be trapped. There often seems to be no reason for it. Unless the same mistake is made across the weave, it is not the fault of the selection system. My guess is that just occasionally the weaving yarn fails to make contact with the weaving brushes fairly and squarely, and the yarn slips out and floats where it should not. We can repair the odd mistake neatly with a needle threaded in the base yarn.

30 Card for Fig. 28

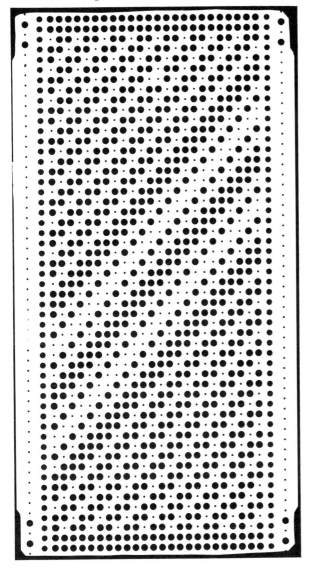

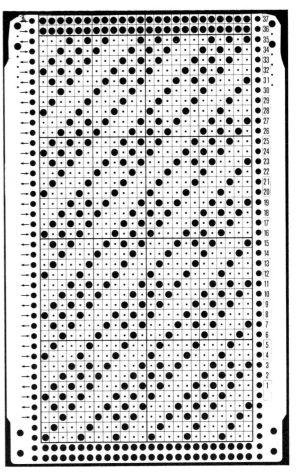

31 Card for Fig. 29

▲ 32 Horizontal chevrons counterchanged into diamonds

▼ 33 Vertical chevrons

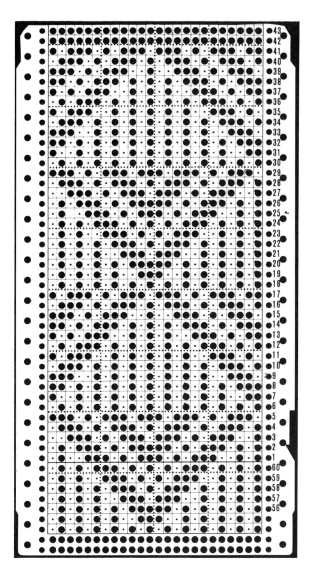

34 Card for Fig. 32

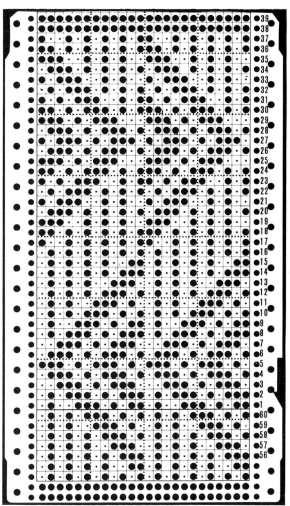

35 Card for Fig. 33

▲ 36 Elongated patterns from Figs. 32 and 33   ▼ 37 Treble chevrons (reverse side of fabric)

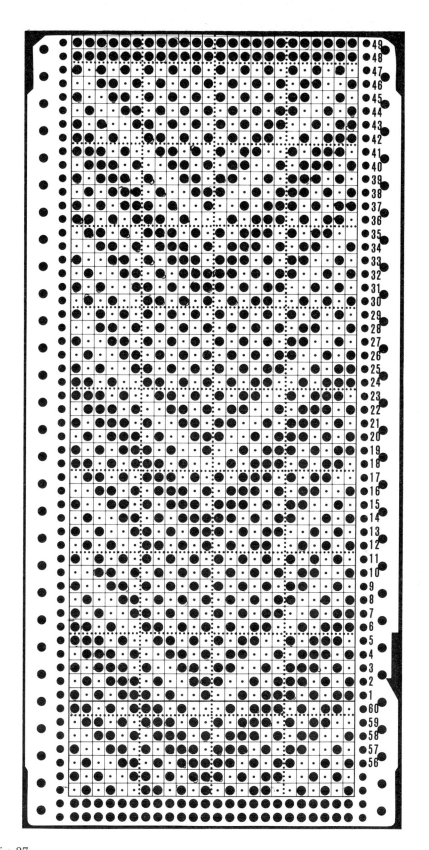

▲ 39 Collection of chevrons

▼ 40 Vertical pillars and mini chevrons

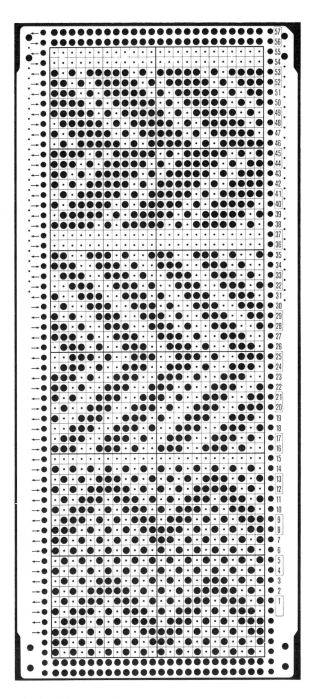

41 Card for Fig. 39

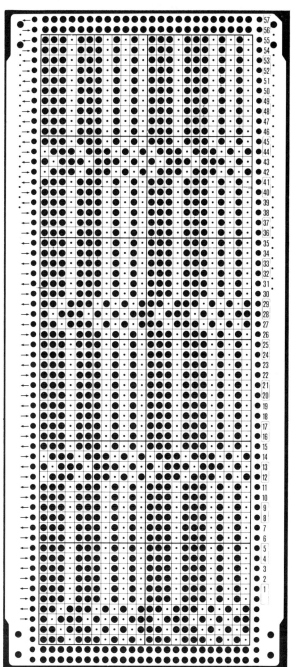

42 Card for Fig. 40

51

▲ 43 Knitmaster 305 chevron patterns translated from a photograph

▼ 44 Small hexagons and diamonds with a colour change

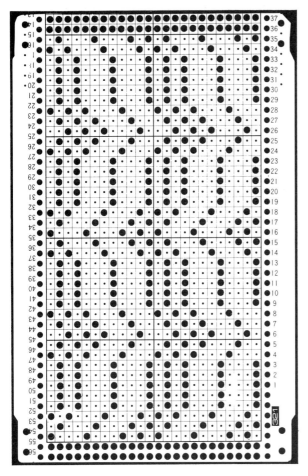

45 Card for Fig. 43

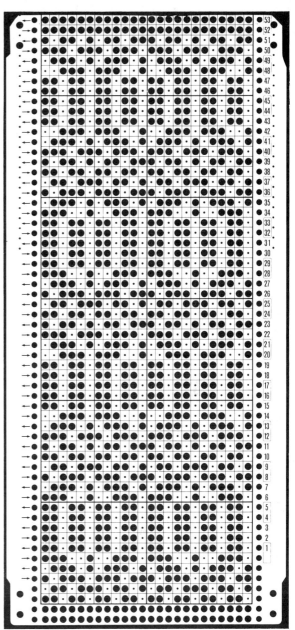

46 Card for Fig. 44

53

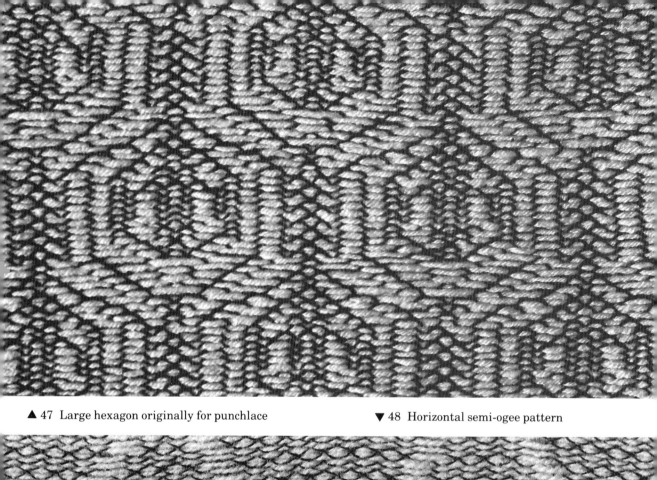

▲ 47 Large hexagon originally for punchlace

▼ 48 Horizontal semi-ogee pattern

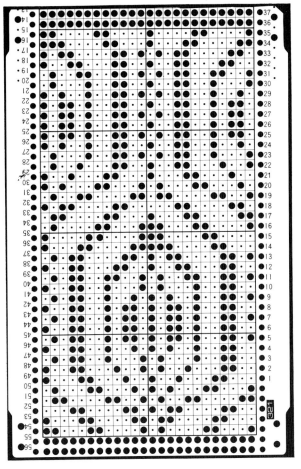

49 Card for Fig. 47

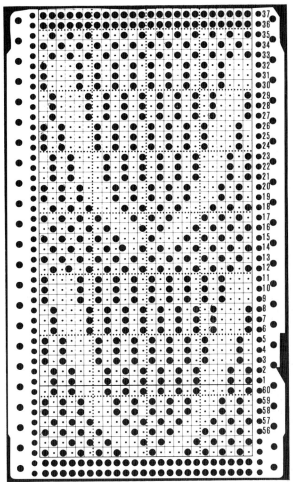

50 Card for Fig. 48

▲ 51 Vertical semi-ogee pattern. Note horizontal line   ▼ 52 Full ogee with different weave backgrounds

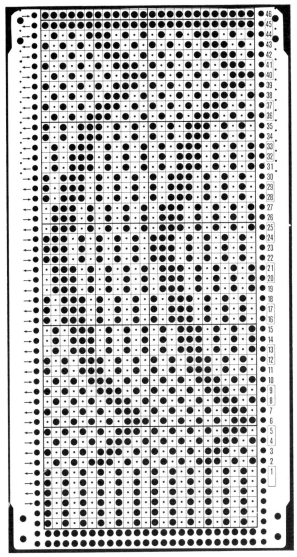

53 Card for Fig. 51

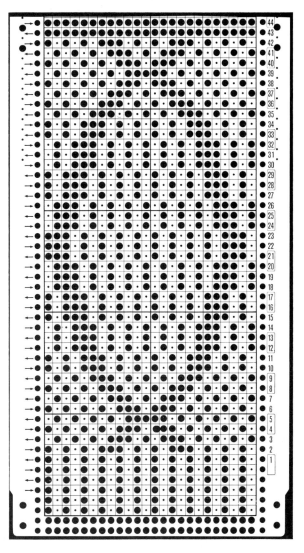

54 Card for Fig. 52

▲ 55 Full ogee with Card 1 ORR background   ▼ 56 Double cable with cut floats

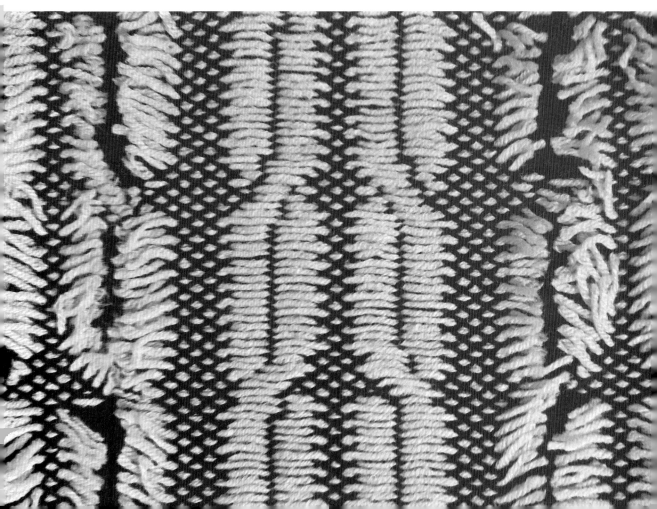

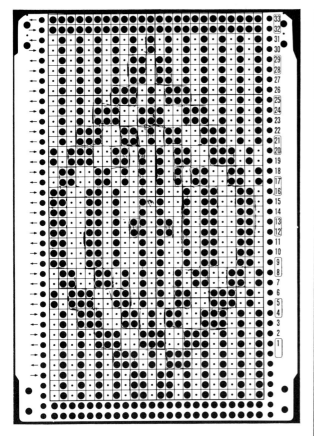

57 Card for Fig. 55

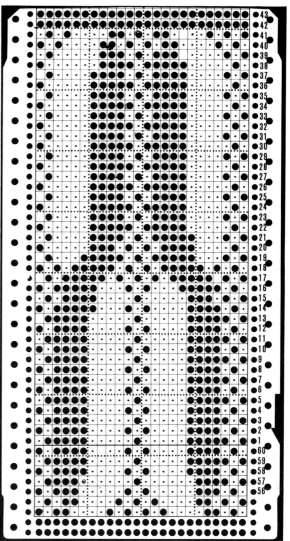

58 Card for Fig. 56

59 Basketweave translated from a lined jacquard
pattern

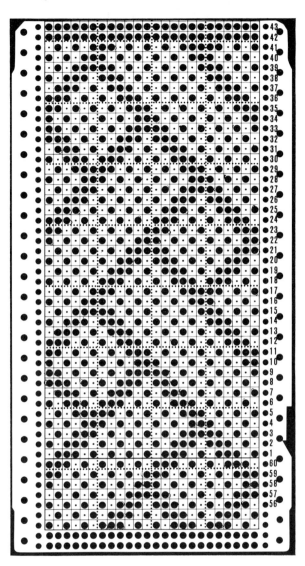

60 Card for Fig. 59

5 Bands, borders and special knitweave effects

Bands or welts

Knitweave, like tuck, has fewer stitches per 10cm (4in) than stocking stitch. It has more rows per 10cm (4in) than stocking stitch, but usually not as many as tuck stitch. The stitch situation, in particular, has a bearing on the welts one can use. Because the industrial 2x2 rib has a third more stitches in its complement, it is a good choice to accompany a knitweave main fabric, though, of course, the 1x1 tends to remain the favourite. The usual 2x1 single-bed welt, knitted double, is fine, but it should be knitted a whole number looser than normal to cope with the shortage of stitches. We need to remember that knitweave is mostly a purl side right side fabric (again like tuck), and therefore the sealing row on any double hem or welt is going to show.

You need to think out very carefully what effect is best for the garment you have in mind. It may be better to stitch down the hem by hand. In that case, you can begin to knitweave from the fold row of the hem. You could turn the first half of the hem, or the whole of it on the garter bar or on waste yarn, so that you have a purl side, knitwoven hem section that is joined on the right side (purl). An attractive hem is one that it begun on every other needle in waste yarn first. After the first row of main yarn has been knitted, re-introduce the NWP needles to make up the full complement and carry on knitting the hem. Knit one row fewer than usual, and on the final row pick up every other loop onto alternate needles. Knit the row and you have an attractive, lacy sealing row to your hem.

As far as sideways knitted garments are concerned, one has to add the bottom welt and cuffs afterwards. Indeed it is often better to begin the main piece (which is knitted conventionally) using waste yarn, and then join the piece to the welt which is knitted later. Alternatively, one can knit thread elastic into the welts. There are three main reasons for adding the welts on completion of knitting:

1. An attractive blouson effect is the result.

2. A firm, elasticated welt lessens the risk of the garment elongating because of its high row count. It could drop after the first wash if it is not laundered with care.

3. A welt added later removes the problem of a first non-patterning row.

In a double hem or welt, for example, it is difficult to close the hem, and have the row pattern at the same time. In a normal rib situation, it is easier, but one must still memorise or select before one can knitweave the row.

If the half-pitch 2x2 industrial rib is used, then one must remember that one cannot pick up the stitches and loops round the neck or wrist in this formation. Therefore, one uses the full pitch alternative, or either 2x1 (the 1 on the ribber), or 2x2, where each stitch or loop is matched exactly to an opposite NWP needle.

Sampling border patterns

Before I collected the borders together on one card, I had them all on bits of card offcuts; incidentally, most are suitable for Fair Isle. A border pattern or two, breaking across an allover weave, can lift the garment into a special category, especially if the garment is sideways knitted.

I used a background of white, 2-ply acrylic, T4 on the Brother 881, while the inlay yarns were bits and pieces of left-overs. I move between machines to do my work, and must remember to mark the first row on the Knitmaster punchcard machine 5 clear rows up, and on the Brother and Toyota, 7 clear rows up from the bottom.

Because of the stitch and row relationship, one can never be sure what knitweave patterns will

61 Borders on a sampler

look like when they are knitted up. The shape will certainly be more squat than its appearance on the card. The first thing to do is to knit the patterns mindlessly, one after the other, separating each pattern with two or three plain rows, locking the card or switching off the pattern while one does so. On completion, study the sample, jot down which you prefer, and suggest a purpose. Can you develop any of the border patterns into a full-sized one?

Knitweave in conjunction with other stitch patterns

In the top half of the swatch (*Fig. 61*), beginning with the black border, I used some of the same patterns, but incorporated tuck, slip, reversed Fair Isle or lace, locking the card and altering the patterning cams as required. The results are quite spectacular, with strong, textural

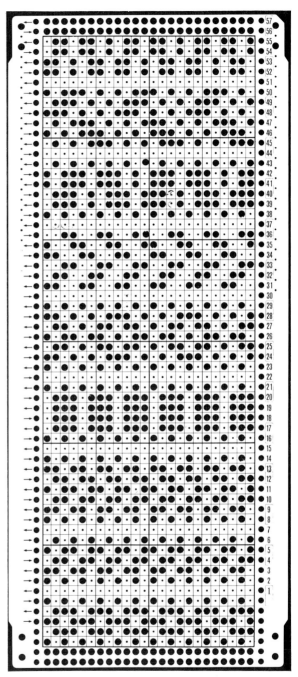

62 Card for Fig. 61

qualities very appealing to the sense of touch. Study your border patterns and decide where you could introduce another stitch effect.

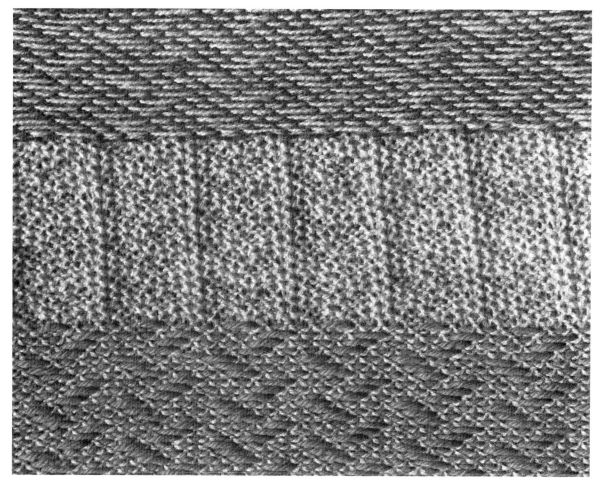

63 Multipurpose pattern: (*bottom*) weave,
(*centre*) tuck, (*top*) FI reversed

Tuck stitch

On the card (*Fig. 62*), note the rows of 1x1, 1x2
or 1x3 repeats, where one blank has a hole or
blank on each side. (Electronics: do not use
reversal in this situation.) Tuck stitch on either
side of the border throws it up into relief, and
alters the shape of the pattern. Compare the two
patterns knitted in black, and you will see the
difference. Tuck is good to use with knitweave.
Its stitch count is similar, even if its row count is
greater, and that is why you get an extra three-
dimensional quality when you use weave and
tuck in conjunction. When tuck is used in the
middle of knitweave, however, it forms a hollow
which can be a very striking feature in a skirt.

Slip stitch

There is an attractive slip stitch produced from
the 1x1 pattern on a locked row which we call
the tea-cosy pattern or ridge stitch. I have used
8 rows slip, 2 rows stocking stitch to frame the
arrow-shaped chevron, knitweave pattern. This
combination pattern of slip and knitweave is a
new discovery, at least for me. I am delighted
with it. It can appear in all kinds of situations,
generally to make the knitweave more
interesting. One use certainly is to highlight
long vertical top seams from neck to wrist in
some sideways knitted garments.

Reversed Fair Isle

The pattern is the fourth one from the bottom of
the card. The straightforward knitweave
version is the fourth from the bottom of the
sample, but the one under discussion is the third
from the top. I locked the card for an ORR

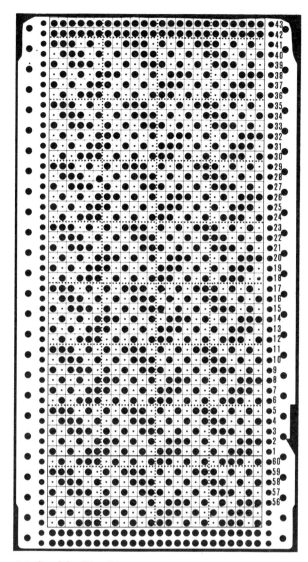

64 Card for Fig. 63

pattern, and used chenille (deep wine) as the inlay. This is a favourite yarn with knitweavers. It is very expensive even on cone, but if you use it tastefully, in small amounts, it can give a garment a very special appeal.

The reversed Fair Isle in 4-ply maroon and grey-blue has a quite different look from the surrounding knitweave. Again it bubbles above the knitweave. Reversed Fair Isle has a lower row count and slightly higher stitch count than the knitweave, and so its absorption into the knitweave framework is bound to give a slight bubble effect, which is most attractive and useful in so many situations. Reversed Fair Isle

is a denser fabric than knitweave and is therefore warmer.

As we have already observed, a reversed Fair Isle jacket and a matching knitweave skirt make good co-ordinates. I first saw this combination used very effectively in a Lois Franklin collection. A mohair weft used with Hobby as base was another Lois Franklin inspiration.

It is unfortunate that in the UK we can only think of the most innovative knitters as those who have a 'London connection'. Lois Franklin has no such connection. There must be many more like her whose genius goes unrecognised by the official arbiters of fashion. Well-publicised craft fairs, the involvement of the tourist industry and the emergence of regional fashion centres are steps in the right direction. Finally, designers who earn their living by their talents do not publish their secrets. This is why it is rather important that a historical assessment be made in an attempt to give innovators the recognition due to them.

Lace

The Brother and the Toyota machines are capable of the most beautiful knitweave and lace combinations, producing sophisticated pattern shapes. Woven lace in all its forms is a subject in its own right. Here we are concerned primarily with the knitweave effect and other stitches which can be its ancillaries. The lace I discuss in this book is mostly the basic 1x1, which is very easy to transfer by hand. You can certainly use your lace carriage to speed up the process (Brother and Toyota), or if the cams on the lace carriage have been memorised before-hand (Knitmaster). Lace again has a low stitch and row count compared with knitweave, and since it is well known for its draping qualities, it is an obvious choice for a skirt. On the border next to the top, I locked the card and framed the knitweave at the bottom and the top with a 1x1 lace which provided a superb spatial contrast with the knitweave.

Special knitweave effects
The cut float technique (Figs. 65 and 68)

When this technique first appeared in *Modern Knitting* in the late 1970s, we were advised to tape over sections of the card so that the inlay

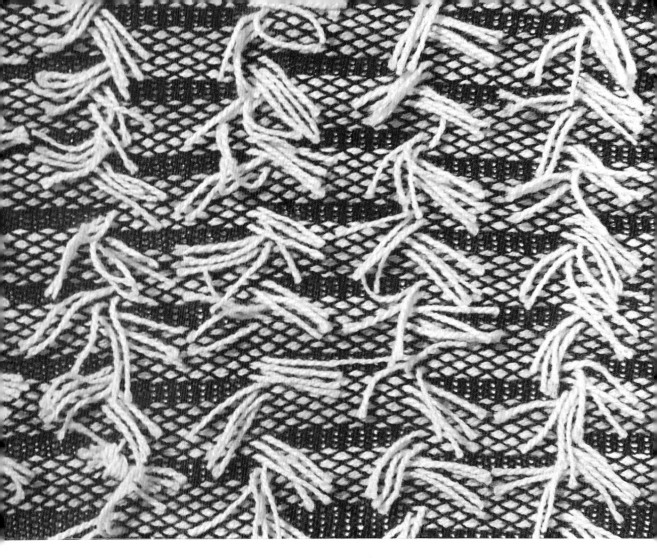

65 Rectangular weave pattern and cut floats

could float underneath the non-selected needles, as represented by the tape on the covered area of the card. Here I have designed a dual purpose card, which will not only do for the cut float approach, but which can be used to illustrate panel or motif knitweave. It is important, however, to bear in mind that cut floats draw out very easily and they cannot be replaced, so you need a card with a fair expanse of pattern to hold the floats in position. I used a strand of 2/30s acrylic (black), on T3 on the Knitmaster 700, and 4-ply acrylic with peach and grey as the inlay yarns. The grey was for the allover weave, and the peach for the cut float sections. You need to cut the floats centrally. Brush or fluff them for interest if you choose. Incidentally, this pattern is most attractive on the reverse side.

Motif or panel knitweave (Brother and Toyota) (Figs. 66 and 68)

I used a double strand of 2/24s grey botany as the base, and a variegated red, black and fuchsia 4-ply as the inlay. The tension was 3.1 on the Toyota 901 (elongated pattern). You will require a separate ball of yarn for each of the knitweave panels (here only four sections), and you lay the yarn over the selected needles. The motifs are, of course, on a stocking stitch background, and again look good on the reverse side. (**NB** You can do a single motif in knitweave on the Knitmaster quite easily.)

Intarsia knitweave (Fig. 66)

There are two versions:

1. Using HP needles. This can be done on all Japanese single-bed machines, since the pattern is controlled and directed by the holding

▲ 66 Panel and motif knitweave from Fig. 68

▼ 67 Sample showing tapestry weave pattern and geometric intarsia

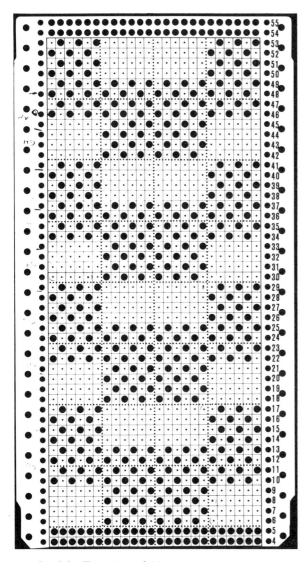

68 Card for Figs. 65 and 66

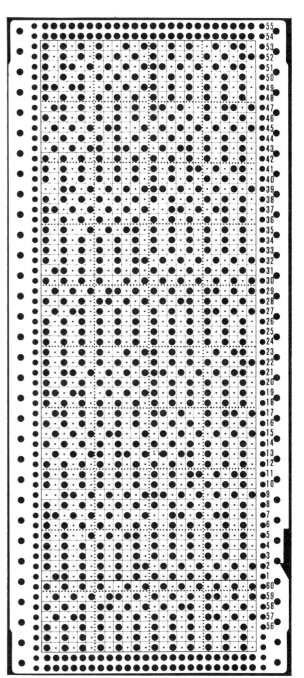

69 Free-style card for Fig. 67 (top)

of needles and their progressive re-introduction into WP. We can, of course, work any simple geometric pattern based on diagonals. This method is an excellent way of introducing arrow-shaped, coloured wedges or stripes into flared, sideways knitwoven garments. The knitter needs to plan the colour changes beforehand. One must be careful to close the gap between the last HP needle and the first WP one (*see Chapter 8*).

2. Free-style intarsia knitweave (Brother and Toyota). This is similar to the more popular stocking stitch intarsia, but is much easier to do. I am tempted to call this technique tapestry knitweave, since there are many similarities with the loom woven counterpart, but since intarsia is in our vocabulary, we will stay with it. I have explored three techniques with the greatest interest, as I realised what untapped

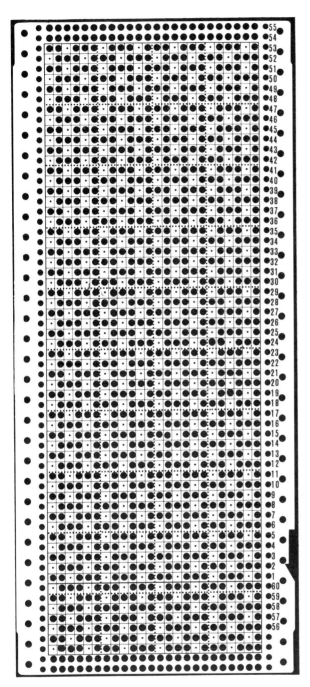

70 Card for tapestry weave (Fig. 67, *bottom*)

potential there is for fibre art expression, providing we can free ourselves from our present preoccupation with 'fashion'.

(i) David Holbourne's *Book of Machine Knitting* contains an interesting section on intarsia knitweave. The card used appears to be a free-style pattern. I also designed my own, using a background of 1x1 ORR pattern, interrupted by 'blisters' of the 1x1 rolling repeat, plus a few scatterings of 2 and 3 stitch span floats (*Fig. 69*). The intarsia needles were hand-fed in a diagonal progression. I used three colours of DK yarn – pale pink, dark green and spring green – on a backing yarn of one strand of 2/30s (T3.1, Brother 881). I laid the yarns over the needles, but did not overlap them, in order to achieve a crisp edge to the pattern.

(ii) The tapestry knitweave card (*Fig. 70*) provided me with a fascinating exercise. The pattern it produces, 3x1 on a 2 row repeat, reminds me of tapestry weave. I discovered that by pushing back every alternate needle within the dark green diamond, and selecting the card 1 ORR pattern, I had created a most interesting contrast of shape, colour and texture, and the edges were clear and sharp.

(iii) For this method (*Fig. 72*) I used a transparent nylon, monofilament yarn as base (T2 on the Toyota 901), and the basic 1x1 ORR pattern. I found the nylon to be remarkably versatile. It is very strong, and allows quite heavy yarns to be knitwoven on this low tension setting. I laid over the yarns at random, leaving the background uncovered in places. This technique gives a disembodied, almost ethereal quality to the weft yarns. They appear to float on an invisible web, and the shapes can be as interesting and as varied as you like. Moreover I found I did not have to lay over the same yarns every row. I could leave them for a couple of rows, introduce others, and then return to those below. The transparency of the backing allows for much greater freedom than if I had used an opaque base. In pictorial work, the owner of a Brother machine and full-size knitleader has the advantage.

How to deal with loose ends: I have watched tapestry weavers at the Edinburgh Tapestry Company working away at their warp amidst a mass of dangling threads. Machine knitters would find this situation too irritating, and so here I outline a good and speedy method. First trim the ends and, using the work tool, pull the trimmed, loose ends through to the wrong side. Do not attempt to thread each end through the eye of a needle. The work tool used as a weaving

69

71 Lois Franklin. Dress in Intarsia Knitweave
with graduated skirt pattern (Brother 840) (courtesy
Lois Franklin Designer Knitwear)

72 Free-style intarsia using transparent nylon as base

tool is much more efficient and you will be surprised how quickly you can accomplish the tidy-up operation. (Book for inspiration: *The Batsford Book of Tapestry Weaving* by Alec Pearson.)

Looped, tucked and smocked knitweave (Figs. 73 and 74)

The first pattern at the bottom of the swatch was not, I feel, a success (2 rows weaving, 4 rows tuck). The colours (pink) were too closely associated, and it would have been better if I had elongated the pattern to 4 rows weave and 8 rows tuck. I used the Knitmaster 700 at T3, and though I changed the background yarns, none was heavier than 2-ply.

The manual tucking, twisting and winding of weave floats is not in the Knitmaster tradition, yet it is just as easy to do these interesting patterns on a Knitmaster as on a Brother or Toyota machine. According to the old pattern books, there are four kinds of manual weaves:

(i) You lift the floats, spanning at least 3 stitches on the completion of a sequence, on to a central needle (patterns 2 and 3 on the swatch and card).

73 Looped, tucked and smocked knitweave

(ii) You twist one or more floats under or over the others. This gives a smocked effect (pattern 4 on the card, and my favourite). Patterns 3 and 4 are my designs.

(iii) The butterfly wing patterns are very attractive. You lift one float in each repeat, row by row in a staggered sequence, beginning at row 5 and completing the operation 4 blank rows above the first pattern. You begin by hooking the yarn on the first needle to the right of the selected one. This pattern is an adaptation of a Brother one, and it should have 7 blank rows between each sequence. I locked the card and counted. There will be 3 knit rows with no floats to lift before the beginning of the second pattern. I used a 2-ply bouclé (Astrakan) as a background (T5), and a 3-ply wool as the weft. When you lift the float, be sure you have selected the correct one to hook on to the needle.

(iv) The winding round method is very interesting to do. The one row inlay on the dress in Fig. 75 is synthetic ribbon and wound round

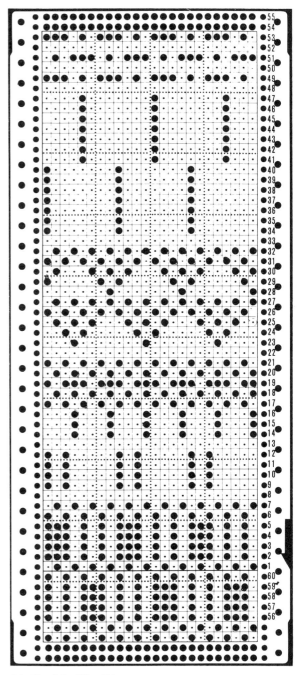

74 Card for Fig. 73

selected needles by hand. The dress, by the way, is knitted in one end of Hobby. Note its superb draping qualities in stocking stitch. The dress is made up entirely by Fig. of 8 and stocking stitch grafts, and is an excellent example of seamless robe knitting (*see Chapter 7*).

75 Dress by Gwen Merrick showing winding round
technique

On the Knitmaster, lock the card a row at a time, and select the needles manually according to the grey touch levers. Push the needles to D position, side levers forward and weaving brushes down. Wind the inlay yarn over the isolated needles, under and over the groups of three all along the row. Then knit the row. This technique provides a good contrast and can bring a refreshing change to an allover bland weave. Try separating the rows with more plain knitting. (Knitmaster 560, put the cam lever to 0 as for the weaving cast on method.)

Lacy knitweave (for mohair) (Figs. 76 and 77)

I mention mohair specifically because it remains a firm favourite with the teens and twenties, but any heavy yarn can be knitwoven in this way. In the sample, I used one strand of Hobby as the base, since Hobby and mohair co-ordinate perfectly. There are other similar yarns you can use. The weft is grey kid mohair with a deep and luxurious hairy pile. For this approach you must take back some needles to NWP (T8, Brother 881). There is, however, one exception on the card. We begin to discuss the samples from the bottom upwards.

Patterns 1 and 2 – place every alternate needle in NWP.

Pattern 3 – no needles in NWP. This is a very interesting open pattern, good for heavy yarns and plating, and more impressive in knitweave than Knitmaster card 2 from which it was developed (T9).

Pattern 4 – card 1 is my favourite for lacy knitweave. Take back pairs of needles to NWP, leaving 2 in WP, 2 in NWP etc.

Pattern 5 – card 1 elongated is Knitmaster card 7. Treat as pattern 4.

76 Lacy knitweave with mohair weft

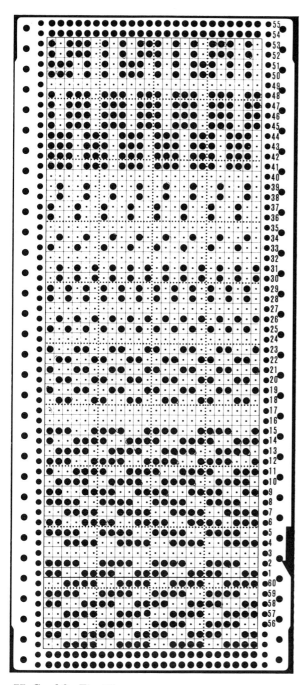

77 Card for Fig. 76

Pattern 6 – take the first needle to the left of 0 on the bed, and every following third needle to NWP.

Pattern 7 – as number 6.

Pattern 8 – Knitmaster card 3. Take every alternate needle, beginning with the first needle to the left of 0, to NWP or every fourth needle on the right of 0 to NWP.

Pattern 9 – take the first needle to the left of 0 and every following fourth needle to NWP.

Note for Brother owners with the newer punchcard machines: remember to alter the orange cams under the carriage as per manual. Brother 910 – use KCII.

Plated knitweave

Knitweave and plating are an excellent combination. Use two fine yarns as the base; the lighter of the two is better in the plating feeder. The weft yarns can be 4-ply to DK in weight. You can indeed achieve some stunning effects. Try plating a 2/30s acrylic (black), with a silver lurex thread. Use a black shiny crêpe or a velvety chenille as the inlay yarn. Choose a pattern that allows the plated base yarn to glint subtly in the background. You will be surprised at the beauty of the fabric.

Embroidery effects

The knitweave surface is excellent for hand embroidery, which is, of course, traditional. Try first to embroider around a clearly defined outline, like a diamond or oval, using simple stitches like stem, cross and chain (*Figs. 78 and 80*). Clusters of French knots and bullion stitches can also be very effective.

Pastel dye sticks

These sticks are a recent innovation introduced to us by Iris Bishop, and knitters are beginning to use them on Fair Isle patterns. I am delighted with my first knitweave sample dyed in this way, but I did find that the floats required a lot of stick, and therefore this process could prove an expensive one. It certainly works, and a new dimension is introduced into our knitweave patterns.

Beading

I have been interested in applying beads to machine knit fabric for many years. If in the early days I was stitching beads on to fabric, then by 1982 I was knitweaving them in on transparent nylon thread. I felt that some way ought to be found of slipping beads over the

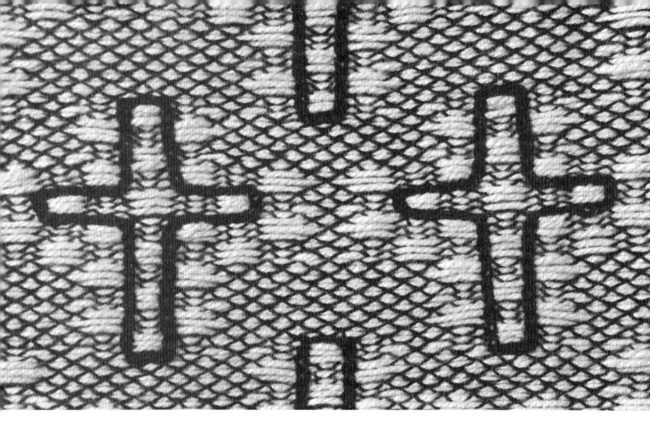

▲ 78 Embroidered cross for a church kneeler

▼ 79 Beading

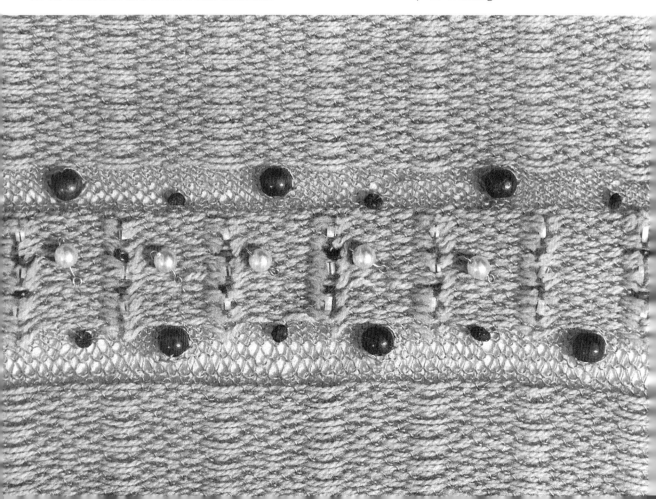

stitches, but I had no tool to enable me to do it.

A few months ago, I had a faulty double-eyed bodkin, which had a split in the metal surrounding one of its eyes. Instead of throwing the bodkin away, I filed the broken metal down to fashion an opening, and therefore, a hook. I now have a tool which serves as an excellent beading hook.

I take the stitch off on to the bodkin by inserting the perfect eye into the latch of the needle. The stitch slides down the shank of the tool into the hook at the bottom. I then slip a bead along the tool and over the opposite end. The bead firmly encircles the stitch, which is lifted up and replaced easily on the needle. The bead is exposed equally on both sides of the fabric. The tension and yarn must be suitable, and the beads one chooses must have a wide enough opening.

In the sample (*Fig. 79*) I have used Atlas wooden beads, chopped pieces of plastic straw, and ring beads from a necklace bought for a few pence at a jumble sale. When beads are too large, or are in danger of being damaged by the carriage, you can undo the stitch while you bead it or knit two rows by hand. Alternatively, you can prepare the beads by tying a noose of main yarn through each one. Hang the noose over the tool and the stitch. The bead then falls down below the danger line. After two rows of pattern, remove the stitch on the tool and pick up the noose behind. Hang it on the needle before replacing the stitch. The bead is now securely anchored and is visible only on the purl side. This method is excellent when you want to show a large bead or a decorative button with a pattern stitch immediately behind it.

While one can employ beading on all kinds of machine knit fabric, the contrast provided by knitweave adorned with beads is particularly successful. Please note that the above technique for beading was described in Alles Hutchinson's *News and Views* (USA) Vol. 9 No. 5 (1979). It is clearly illustrated in *A Machine Knitter's Guide to Creating Fabrics* (Susanna Lewis, Julia Weissman, 1986). In both publications, the tool recommended is a fine crochet hook. The double-eyed bodkin is too thick to take the new Japanese beads imported to the UK by BSK, but a tapestry needle with its eye filed to a hook is an excellent tool.

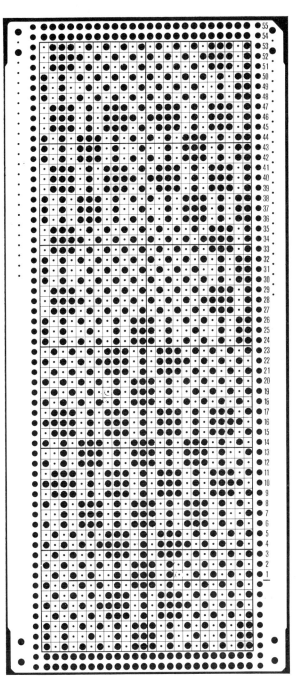

80 Card for Fig. 78

77

Cords and bobbles

Cords

The application of cords on knitwear has been a popular fashion for a long time with Brother designers. In the December 1985 edition of *Hello Knit* there was a distinctive, sideways knitted sweater, with cords arranged and stitched down in various cable formations on areas of reversed stocking stitch between bands of knitweave. The partnership of cords and knitweave was very striking indeed.

Bobbles

These can be knitted manually anywhere you want. Select 3 to 5 needles and knit 6 to 10 rows manually with a contrast yarn. Take the stitches on to a bodkin. With your free hand and a transfer tool, pick up the loops at the back of the knitting from the first row of contrast yarn. Put these loops on the needles first before you replace the ones on the bodkin.

Ruching

Ruching is very much in favour at the moment. It mostly concerns bands of stocking stitch or Fair Isle in contrasting colours, and the manual picking-up of key stitches so many rows below, to create a bubble formation on the knit side and an in-depth hollow on the purl. Apart from the three-dimensional effect, colours seen in shadow cast a different hue than they do when they are observed on a flat surface.

Mary Farrin is a well-known designer who has frequently incorporated knitweave sections in her garments. More recently, she has used the ruching techniques very effectively in total look ensembles in overall knitweave.

To create a fabric supple enough for picking up, it is important to choose an inlay yarn no heavier than the base. You can achieve some beautiful contrasting effects in colour and texture. In this situation, the ruching is observed on the purl side.

Knitweave and English rib

In Mary Weaver's *The Ribbing Attachment*, Part 1, there are several very interesting patterns in English or Half-fisherman's rib, decorated with bands of knitweave. The garments are knitted conventionally and the knitweave appears as horizontal bands. The contrast is unusual and attractive. It is important that the main bed be set to tuck, and not the ribber, which knits normally. Use a 1x1 setting with a 3-ply yarn as the main and DK as weft.

6 The edging principle and summer knitweave

Single thickness edgings, as distinct from ribbed and double stocking stitch bands, are best used on light- to medium-weight knitwoven garments to decorate necklines, pocket tops, short sleeve and front edges. Edgings can be made direct onto selvages where stitch loops are picked up in such a way that they hide the weave floats at the edge. Stitches held on waste yarn, as on sleeve edges and on sideways knitted central wedges (jackets and V necks), can also be used as a base. On V necks, lace holes form in the same way as they do when we hold stitches on a diagonal for an all-in-one raglan. We can choose to highlight or hide them by the edging we construct.

There are four initial considerations regarding the edging principle.

1. We choose the colour of the edging to tone in with the main garment pieces. The basic rule is that if the main fabric is multi-coloured and has a sophisticated surface pattern, then we choose a simpler border than we would if the main fabric were self-coloured in an allover ORR weave. In the latter case, we might choose an edging in a similar colour but in a different texture – shiny to contrast with matt, for example.

2. The weight of the edging must be balanced against the weight of the fabric, and a trial on the edge of your tension swatch will show whether your edging is too thin and floppy, too strong and heavy, or just right. An edging must complement the main fabric. It must not undermine or overpower it.

3. Consider the stitch and row ratio of the main fabric. Overall knitweave has around a 1-1.75, 1-2 or even a 1-3 ratio. You find the ratio by reducing the stitches and rows per 10cm (4in) to their lowest common denominators. Therefore, 32 stitches and 48 rows have a ratio of 2-3; 28 stitches and 40 rows – 3.5-5; 23 stitches and 45 rows (knitweave ratio) is 1-2 to the nearest whole number. In the latter case, you would pick up 1 stitch loop out of 2 at the edge, counting the knots as loops, since they represent a row of knitting.

4. Consider the stitch you are going to use in the edging. If it is knitweave or tuck, then the ratio is comparable to that in the main piece. Try picking up 1 out of 2, 2 out of 3, or even 3 out of 4 loops. It also depends on the tuck ratio. If stocking stitch is used, then you pick up virtually every loop at the edge (no knots). This approach works well on straight horizontal or vertical edges, but on a diagonal it is not quite so easy. Usually I find I need 4 to 6 stitches more than the ratio suggests, to accommodate the slope.

Because of the WY wedge method I suggest for sideways knitted V necks, the stitches are already held and ready to be knitted into an edging. In that case, you must consider very carefully the stitch pattern you can use on that edging. Single thickness edgings can produce problems if they warp or fail to lie flat. They can consequently pull the neckline out of shape. A consideration of the mathematics involved, and then a trial run, will avoid a lot of frustration, no matter what edgings or bands are employed in the finishing process.

It is an indication of the versatility of the machine knitting craft and of the rich diversity of human talent that so many different interpretations of knitting subjects can be worked out and presented. On the other hand, it is intriguing to find out how often knitters arrive at the same or similar conclusions quite independently. It would therefore be very foolish to claim that one is first on the worldwide scene with any knitting method, technique or approach.

81 Lois Franklin 'Monet' Italian space-dyed mohair woven on viscose to produce an ultra-lightweight fabric. Skirt is more than a full circle (courtesy Knitting International)

The edging technique

I devised and published my approach to edgings several years ago. I was particularly keen to find a technique whereby the stitches stayed on the needles for the whole of the edging, thereby increasing the speed of execution. At the same time, since single-thickness, stocking stitch-based fabrics are apt to twist and warp, I had to find methods to prevent this. A number of edgings are given for you to try, but first, here are the two key areas of casting on and casting off.

Casting on

1. The crochet cast on chain method is vital to this approach; indeed, I use it more than any other in this book. If we want a knit-side edging to appear on the purl side, right side of the main garment, then we put the crochet cast on chain on the needles *before* we pick up the edge loops. If the edging is to be purl side, right side, then the crochet cast-on goes on *after* we pick up the edge loops.

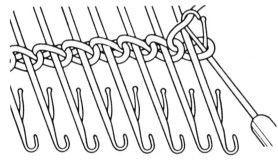

82 Crochet cast on (chain method)

Method. Begin by tying a slip knot of main yarn, and slipping it like a noose over the latch head of the work tool. Start at the opposite end to the carriage. Do not have the yarn in the carriage feed. Poke the tool, head pointing upwards and looped with the noose, between needles 1 and 2. Bring the yarn over needle 1, and grasp it with the work tool, drawing the yarn through. Slip off the noose, and you have a new loop in the latch head. Now go along the row between needles 2 and 3, then 3 and 4 and so on, repeating the chain-making process. Slip the loop on the tool onto the last needle of all. Practice makes perfect, and speed comes with experience.

I have found that you can poke the tool down from above the needles and grab the yarn below. This makes a different, but very attractive upside-down chain. You can also bring the edging stitches forward on the needles during or at the end of the knitting process, in order to work a chain behind; but be careful not to pull the stitches off the needles. This technique requires practice, but it is well worth the effort.

The whole purpose of a chain laid at the foundation of the edging is to provide a crisp, clean line, which is a stabilising influence on the edging which rises above it. **NB** Two other names for the work tool are the latch tool and the tappet tool.

2. The e wrap cast on is known to everyone. I use this occasionally as an alternative to the crochet chain cast on method. It makes a refreshing change, but it is nowhere near as versatile nor as stable as the cast on chain, as an edging formation.

Casting off

The last few rows and the final finish can make or break an edging, and are often the deciding factors with regard to whether the edging is going to distort, wave or lie flat.

1. The first stitch on the next stitch is a manual cast off. It is in every instruction book, and is universally known and used. Of all cast off methods it is the least valuable in the total row situation. It is, however, useful for the decrease of small stitch groups, though the cast off stitches are best taken behind the sinker pins to avoid a tight and uneven edge.

A tip from Anne Bayes (Sydney, Australia) is to pass the first stitch across the second stitch on to the third stitch. Go back and cast off the second stitch. Take that cast off loop to the fourth stitch and so on. This gives a most attractive crochet-like edge similar to crab stitch. In this situation you would use the technique for the whole row.

2. The work tool link-off method is very popular, and is the one recommended by several knitweave authorities. Knit one row (occasionally two) on T10 or on the optimum tension (around 8-9 if the yarn is 1-2-ply). Use either the work tool, a crochet hook, or the little Knitmaster or Brother linker to make the final casting off chain. This produces a very straight clean line which does not always co-ordinate

with the weave undulations. Though the method is popular, speedy and versatile to a certain extent, it is not a universal remedy. Indeed, in certain knitweave situations (see instructions for making up sideways knitted tops and skirts, *Chapter 8*), there are better methods to employ.

On stocking stitch, the work tool method turns the chain to the back of the work, i.e. the knit side. What method do we want when we want the chain to the front?

3. The crochet-cast off work tool method is one I have used for many years. An optimum tension row is not needed. The carriage and yarn are at the side you wish to work. Take the yarn out of the carriage feed. Insert the work tool head into the first stitch. Remove the stitch onto the tool and make one loop of a chain by slipping the stitch behind the latch and

allowing the tool to take a bite of yarn. You may make as many chains as you like between the stitches, but you must begin with both the old loop and the newly-removed stitch behind the latch. By this method, you make a chain. On stocking stitch fabric the chain is laid in front and not behind.

Tip on using the work tool. The best way for an even and speedy cast off is to turn the hook head on one side so that the latch will not catch on the stitch. Insert the rounded head into the centre of the stitch, then turn the tool and grasp the loop in the open hook. Uneven casting off can occur when the hook is inserted with the latch uppermost. The latch plucks at the stitch, splits the yarn and makes an irregular, untidy cast off edge with chains of differing lengths.

4. The Fig. of 8 graft (*Fig. 83*). I have explained and illustrated this in previous publications. It is a traditional technique popular in the north-west of England, partly because it is the

83 Starting the Fig. of 8, (reproduced from *Techniques of Machine Knitting* [Kinder])

perfectionist method taught in the region's examination course in machine knitting. No one knows where the Fig. of 8 originated. Its distinctive feature is that it is exclusively a machine knitter's method of casting off by hand on the single bed. It could well have its origins in the eighteenth century; the framework knitters of the period were very proud of their handtooling methods at the machine (though no one seems to know what these were either).

I have discovered that the Fig. of 8 graft is extremely useful, not only for its crochet-like finish in single thickness edgings, but also for the making up of knitweave sections where the join has to be as near invisible and as elastic as possible. This applies to open selvage and diagonal cast off edges. The undulations of the graft can be made to synchronise with the above and below floats in knitweave. If there is a slight gape on the weave side, then the edges can be drawn together with an invisible blind stitch. The following instructions apply to the use of the graft on the last row of an edging.

Method. Pull down and break off a piece of main yarn five times the measurement of the WP needles across the bed (i.e. stitches to be grafted off). Remove the yarn from the carriage feed and push all WP needles to HP.
* Take the first needle back to UWP, loop behind latch. Lay the yarn in the hook head and knit off. With a one-eyed latch tool, approach this loop from behind, coming towards yourself. Take the tool through the loop. Twist the tool over and down and you have the Fig. of 8. Put the half stitch held by the tool onto the next needle, and leave the other half in the first needle until all the loops are grafted off.

The next stage is to slip the second stitch over the top half of the Fig. of 8 in the needle latch head and continue from *. When all stitches have been knitted off, and half Fig. of 8 loops are in every needle in the complement, remove from the machine, after you have fastened off the end of the yarn through the last loop. This is slow to begin with, but speed comes with practice.

5. The ridge stitch finish is one I have just discovered for edgings. This is quick to do, and so beautiful that it must go top of the list. Knit 6 to 8 rows of slip stitch on a locked row of card 1 (1x1 pattern). Knit 1 row main tension stocking stitch, then 1 row optimum tension. Link-latch off. This finish looks good on both the

knit and the purl sides, and gives a firm, stable and also interesting edge.

6. Enclosing the cast off row in a chain stitch strait-jacket is a good way of making a stable and attractive finishing edge. Make two crochet cast on chains, one behind the knitting and the other in front of the last row of the edging. Graft off the loops using the Fig. of 8. The result is very much like a mini crochet frill.

Note on the use of crochet

In the English-speaking world, machine knitters are keen on making machine knit edges that look like crochet, but they rarely do the real thing. Crochet edges are used extensively on machine knitteds in Japan. Indeed, crochet is a good accompaniment to machine knitting, and produces beautiful flat edges which can have infinite variety. Some British knitters say they cannot crochet, which is patently untrue, because every time they do a link latch-off row, they are following a basic crochet procedure. However, crochet on fine knitweave fabric would take a lot longer to do than the edgings I describe here, and you must make your own choice.

Edgings and cut and sew

With the arrival on the knitting scene of domestic overlockers like the Frister Knitlock 5, which are designed specifically to deal with knitted fabrics, there is growing interest in cut and sew. My approach is that of the knitter and not of the sewer. After I have prepared the fabric by pressing or steaming, I cut out and immediately pin and overlock the pieces together without any more ado. Moreover, I have discovered that on fine knitweave one can turn over an overlocked edge, pick up the stitches and apply an edging in exactly the same way as on a shaped edge. The effect is just as beautiful.

There is still an enormous amount of prejudice against cut and sew, which may or may not be historical in origin. In the early nineteenth century, the livelihood of the framework knitters was destroyed by cut and sew methods. Today, however, there is every chance of cut and sew becoming an honourable branch of the craft. Instead of banning it in competitive situations, organisers should set about creating

84 Cord loop trim on neckline

a special cut and sew class. They could be pleasantly surprised at the standard of entries. It is a great pity that at the moment we tend to regard cut and sew not as a first choice technique, but as a second-class remedy in a rescue operation.

The suit of which the neckline is illustrated in Fig. 84 was not intended to be cut and sew. I made a mistake in the weave sequence of the sideways knitted top, abandoned the shaping, and did a straight piece, much more quickly, for cut and sew. I allowed 4mm for the overlocking edge (incidentally, the stitches do not run if you press the fabric). The edging and an alternative are below. I did not even have to stitch down the turned-over edge, and you can hardly see it even though the fabric is very thin.

Cord loop trim

Yarn – Krinklespun (like Hobby, but finer). T2 on the Toyota 901. Set for cord knitting. Right side facing, and with a three-eyed tool * pick up 3 stitches or loops on fold or neck edge, and hitch on needles. Knit 10 rows. Miss a loop on the edge and repeat from *, but place stitches on same needles. Two loops hang on each needle.

Alternative loop trim

As above, but knit stocking stitch with fewer rows in the sequence. Try 6 not 10. Both edgings are very quick to do, and can be applied on neck and cuff edges, jacket fronts and pocket tops, on a completed garment.

The edgings on a summer knitweave sampler (Fig. 85)

I chose the patterns at random. Since I wanted to get the effect of an edging gracing a selvage, I took a piece of summer-weight knitweave, folded it over at intervals, and created an edging on each fold. Edgings are particularly effective on lightweight knitweave where a ribbed or double band would be too heavy. We need to consider, however, the garment we have in mind, whether the edging co-ordinates tastefully with the other features like style of sleeve, neckline and so on. Here we also use edgings as practice pieces for techniques which

85 Edgings on sampler

are indispensable to the correct knitting and making up of knitweave fabric; and by 'correct' I mean the most efficient, expedient and attractive. I discuss the edgings from the top of the sampler downwards, and the machine used was the Brother 881.

Tuck and roll (top)

The yarn was 2x2/24s bright acrylic, plated and using Brother card 3D on tuck. With right side facing, hitch loops on needles and put a crochet chain in front. T4. Knit 8 rows. Crochet cast off with work tool, doing extra chain between needles. **NB** The chain here was turned by the tuck stitch to the back. The edging is very successful and just right for the weight of fabric. (Edging yarn approx 3-ply.)

Seed stitch

Seed stitch is the bottom pattern on the tuck-stock card (*Fig. 86*). The stocking stitch rows separating the tuck stitch sequences create a bumpy, interesting pattern on the knit side, so you can take your choice. Here we have the wrong side of the fabric facing, as we do indeed want a knit-side edging. Do a crochet cast on chain on the needles, then pick up the edge loops. Knit 1 row on T5, but pattern 6 rows on T4 with 2x2/24s bright acrylic. Knit the last row on T10. Link-latch off. Turn the edging and pick up the whole stitch so that the chain lies on top of the needle. T9. Knit 1 row. Link-latch off.

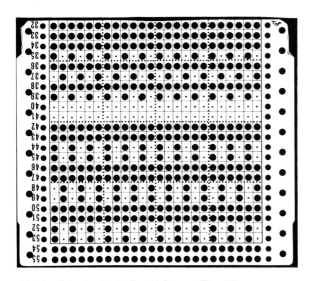

86 Card for tuck-stock stitches on Fig. 85

Weave and roll

Choose a small horizontal chevron from one of the border patterns. Right side facing, pick up loops and use an e wrap in front. Base yarn is 2x2/30s cotton and the inlay yarn 2x2/24s Botany wool. Knit 1 row T5, then on T4, 2 rows tuck, 1 row knit, 4 rows weave. Lock card on 1x1 pattern. 6 rows slip. On T9, knit 1 row. Link-latch off. **NB** You can also slot a fine roueau through the ridge stitch edge.

Mock moss stitch

This is at the top of the tuck-stock card. Yarn: 2x2/24s bright acrylic on T4. Right side facing, pick up loops and put a chain in front. Set to tuck. Knit 8 rows. Put a chain in front and use Fig. of 8 to cast off all loops and stitches.

Lace for rouleau

Make a chain on the needles. With wrong side facing, pick up loops. Yarn: 2x2/24s bright acrylic. On T4, knit 3 rows stocking stitch. Make holes by transferring the 4th and every following 4th stitch to its neighbour. Knit 3 rows stocking stitch. T9, knit 1 row. Link-latch off. Rouleau: 2x2/30s acrylic, T5 over 3 needles. No need to set for cord knitting.

Ridge stitch with Fair Isle

Card 1 locked. Yarn: 2x2/30s cotton and 2x2/30s acrylic. Chain the needles. With wrong side facing, pick up loops. On T4, knit 6 rows Fair Isle. On T5, knit 8 rows slip stitch, 1 row stocking stitch. On T9, knit 1 row. Link-latch off.

Tipped picot (stocking stitch)

This is the only double-thickness edging. Yarn: 2x2/24s bright acrylic. Chain the needles. With wrong side facing, pick up the loops. T4, knit 1 row. T6. Slip every other needle by setting to slip-part-empty, and pushing every other needle forward to HP. Set cams to knit back. T4, knit 4 rows. Change to colour 2. T6. Knit 1 row. Transfer every alternate stitch to its neighbour. Knit 1 row. Change to colour 1. Knit 3 rows.

Pick up slip loops from below onto every other needle. T10. Knit 1 row. Link-latch off.

NB There is no stitching down to do at all, and the reverse side is just as attractive as the right side. The final sealing method has considerable creative use in the making of edges. Do try it on one of your own.

Poke bonnet trim

Chain the needles. With right side facing, pick up the loops. Yarn: colour 1, 1x2/30s acrylic; colour 2, 2x2/24s bright acrylic. T5. With colour 2, knit 1 row. Change to colour 1 and T3. * Push out 4th and every following 4th needle to HP. Set to hold. Knit 6 rows. Push held needles to UWP. Knit 1 row **. Repeat from * to **. T4. Knit to right. Change to colour 2. Using work tool, crochet cast off, making 3 extra chains before and after you pick up the loops from the first row which holds the tuck loops.

Diagonal lace

This is very pretty and delicate, but has a bad bias because of the way the stitches are transferred. On a garment, I would have no scruples about overlocking the edges and cutting off the surplus. If that offends you, choose another lace pattern that does not have this bias problem. Chain first in colour 1 (2x2/24s bright acrylic). T5. Knit 1 row. Change to colour 2 (2x2/24s bright acrylic). T3. Knit 2 rows. * Transfer the 3rd and every alternate stitch to its neighbour. Knit 2 rows and repeat from * till 4 row transfers are complete. Pull needles forward carefully to HP. Pull stitches gently into the latch heads. Hang a claw weight behind. With a spare piece of colour 2 held underneath the fabric, work an upside-down chain from above, over the needles. Change to colour 2. T5. Knit 1 row. Fig. of 8 graft off.

NB Of all the finishes this is surely the most beautiful.

Note on linked and turned edgings

The principle is to knit 1 or 2 optimum tension rows, then link off, turn and pick up again. Though the process is time-consuming, the results are so distinctive and beautiful that one's efforts are rewarded. One interesting approach (from *News and Views*, USA, Vol. 9, No. 5) is to chain the stitches on one of the optimum tension rows across the top of the needles and leave the chains where they are. This effect provides an attractive contrast with a linked and turned row within the same edging.

Note on the Brother garter carriage

One valuable use for the garter carriage is in the area of edgings. Some knitters take edgings off the machine, turn and replace them in order to create a garter stitch structure which is denser, and more stable than stocking stitch. As we have shown here, there is plenty of scope without removing the edgings, but there is no doubt that the garter carriage provides one answer for those who like their edgings turned and replaced.

Two-yarn twisted cast on

Take one end of main, and one end of contrast yarn, or two ends of main or contrast. Begin at the left. Lift yarn 1 over the first needle, twist over yarn 2 underneath. Lift yarn 2 over the second needle and so on. Yarn 1 goes over odd-numbered and yarn 2 over even-numbered needles. This makes an attractive twisted edge. It can also be the basis of an edging after the stitches have been picked up.

Warning: cover your ribber before attempting to edge your garment.

Short row braids (stocking stitch)

If you alternate the HP sequences between the left and the right by separating them with an odd number of straight rows, you get a zig-zag braid (*Fig. 87, top*). If the straight rows are even-numbered, the braid has a peaked scallop along one edge. Here are the instructions for a 4-ply zig-zag braid: cast on by hand 5 stitches. Knit 4 rows. Carriage at right. Set to hold. Push to HP one needle nearest carriage on next and every alternate row 4 times (self-wrap). Knit 1 row. Push last HP needle to UWP on next and every alternate row 4 times. Knit 1 row + 3 rows. Repeat.

Stocking stitch ruffle (Fig. 87)

Bring into WP 14 needles. Take back into NWP the 4th needle from the left, using 2x2/30s acrylic. Cast on by hand over the remainder. T5. Knit 2 rows. Set to hold.* Push 3 needles at extreme left to HP. T3. Knit 4 rows. ** Push 2

87 Ruffle, fringe, applied lace and ric-rac braid

needles to HP. Knit 2 rows. Do not wrap. ***
Repeat from ** to *** 4 times in all. Push back in same sequence for flare. Knit 2 rows etc. Push back 3 needles. Knit 4 rows. Repeat from * to *** for required length. Finishing: pick up neck stitches and loops, right side facing. Hitch ruffle on top. Do chain in front. T6. Knit 1 row. T5. Knit 6 rows ridge stitch and 1 row stocking stitch. T9. Knit 1 row. Link-latch off.

Woven alternative

Use card 1 locked or an ORR card, and knitweave the ruffle, using a 2-ply weft; but first read the techniques in the chapter on skirts. A woven ruffle is a good introduction to the technique of knitweaving flares, and can be an attractive feature on a dress or top.

Woven fringe (Fig. 87, bottom)

Push up 8 needles into WP. Leave 12 needles in NWP in the middle, and push up 2 needles into WP at the right. Card 1. Use 2-ply as main yarn, and 2x4-ply as weft. T6. Set the card to roll. On completion, release and run down the 2 stitches on the right. Cast off the 8 stitches in WP. Steam the fringe to uncurl it, and trim the strands. **NB** You can knitweave a self-coloured fringe, and thicken it by adding yet another strand to the weft.

Applying lace edgings (Fig. 87, centre)

You can knit the edging yourself or buy it. If the edging is commercially made, then you may have to pierce holes along the edge before you can hang it on the needles. Chain the front. Knit a row on T10, and latch off.

7 Seamless robe knitting and the sideways knitwoven top

Seamless robe knitting is a technique of garment knitting and construction and is a most interesting system to employ; but when a choice has to be made between following the technique to the letter, and efficiency and design, I choose efficiency and design every time. In essence, good design is always the most efficient as well as the most aesthetically pleasing approach. Moreover, you can do nearly as good a job far more quickly with the sewing machine, linker or overlocker, than by employing painstaking manual stitch craft.

Machine knitters have been involved in seamless robe knitting ever since the first domestic machines emerged after the Second World War. The machines had holding cams but no automatic patterning. It was soon realised that the holding cams could be used in such a way that all-in-one raglans could be produced whereby back, front and sleeves were knitted as one piece. All that remained to be done was to stitch up the sleeve and side seams and put on the neck band. Since in the north of England the Fig. of 8 graft was used, these garments were as near seamless and tubular as any could be on a single-bed domestic machine.

More recently, one aspect which has aroused lively discussion and controversy is the area of sideways knitting, knitweave in particular. The seamless robe knitter begins and ends with waste yarn any piece that can be grafted invisibly to its other half, i.e. if he or she is determined to follow the technique to the letter. The side seams are grafted by one of the special methods advocated in this chapter. When you come to increase, you use either a hand cast on method or hang a waste swatch of similar weight on the needles and weave straight from there. (A waste swatch is known as a scrap rag in the USA.) The aim is to weave the piece from sleeve cuff to sleeve cuff without any interruption and only stitch a seam that you cannot graft.

Sideways knitwoven tops

As far as tops are concerned, there are four possible options, as listed below.

Option 1

You can weave a half sleeve, back-front, and a half sleeve. Though you have eliminated the sleeve head armhole seam, you are left with a long exposed top seam from neck column to wrist. This approach offers an easy way for both the cut and sew operator and a beginner new to knitweaving a top. Providing the neck is shallow and the shaping at a minimum, the knitweaver has no headaches regarding matching the weave at various break points. I have discovered that we can make a feature out of that long top seam by using a surface weave based on the diagonal. For the second piece, turn over the card and you have a most attractive chevron all down the shoulder line. Another idea is to cover the join with a separately knitted cable or braid. You could choose one of the border patterns edged with ridge stitch (top and bottom). Sew just inside the curls so that the stitches are hidden.

Option 2 (1x1 and ORR patterns)

You can weave the back and front sideways as separate pieces, beginning and ending with waste yarn (WY). You are aiming to get rid of that top sleeve seam and weave a full sleeve width in one go. In stocking stitch there are no real problems, but in knitweave there are. The problems concern (a) which way to weave the sleeve to match the lie of the above and below floats of the weave pattern, and (b) how to seam the sleeve to the main piece at the shoulders and avoid an ugly gap where the two weave structures meet, clash or align. There are two alternatives: we can weave the sleeve separately and seam; or we can pick up the stitches or bottom loops at the shoulder and knit

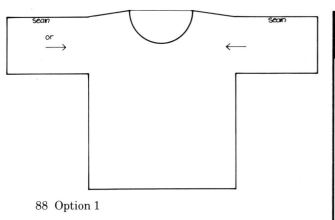

88 Option 1

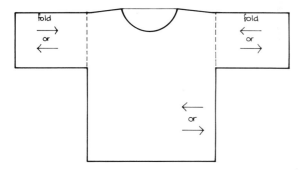

89 Option 2

down. In the case of the bottom loops that come between the first row of stitches, there will be one less than we expect. In each alternative, the weave pattern as we have it on the card will only work for one sleeve. What do we do?

Some suggestions

1. Choose a simple 2 row repeat like card 1. For the back, front and one sleeve, use the card on odd numbers – 1,3,5 – and, during the knitting, move the card on manually every now and again to save wear on that one area. For the second sleeve, which will be knitwoven against the direction of the other pieces, use the card on even numbers – 2,4,6. In other words you are reversing the weave to serve this situation and to ensure that you can use the charting device in the same way as you used it for the first sleeve. I have punched a card (*Fig. 90*) with various ORR weaves designed in two ways (2 rows each), and if you study it, you will see what I mean by reversing the pattern. You can, of course, punch a full length card in the pattern of your choice. Electronics switch to reversal.

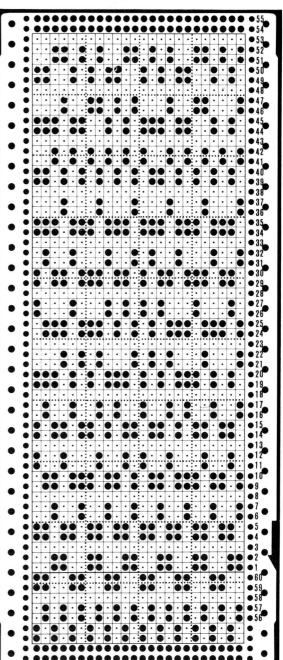

90 Selection of ORR weaves

There is one other very important point. If you are stitching the shoulder seams on the sewing machine then you need to add extra stitches at the appropriate edges and you must mark on the needle rail with indelible felt pen the needle which has to match the centre on the top sleeve. The join needs to be as near faultless as possible,

91 Lois Franklin 'Lysander' Italian viscose and silk
mixture. Note edgings and direction of stripes on
sleeves (courtesy Knitting International)

and a good choice of technique will see that it is. In a pattern more complicated than card 1, I would mark the same needle in each repeat (23 needles between each mark, i.e. every 24th needle), and plan the sleeve on each side of the one nearest to the centre of the bed.

2. A very simple ORR pattern which is unbroken from cuff to cuff can be very boring to look at, and its horizontal lines can seem to stretch interminably across the shoulders and chest. Complicated flechage or arrow-shaped flares of colour are not for the beginner: they need to be planned out carefully beforehand. But one straightforward panel of a different colour, and maybe a change of pattern down one shoulder, can be very flattering, and can hide any ugliness at the seam as well. Have the second pattern begin and end with the main pattern so that the break is not too startling. Alternatively, a simple colour change can be an excellent choice. Cowls are an attractive feature (*Figs. 75 and 81*), and can be worked out by the HP method for a flare. Perhaps the simplest approach is to decorate the neckline itself with an interesting edging (*Fig. 91*).

Option 3

This approach must go nearly to the top of the list for marrying to perfection the techniques of seamless robe knitting with design and efficiency. In fact, I would recommend it in preference to 1 and 2 nearly every time. Except for cut and sew and Option 4, there is no speedier way, and it is certainly an excellent choice for more complicated surface patterns. There are, however, two problems:

1. You cannot weave very deep batwings by this method, because you simply have not got the needles on the bed to cope with the full top width of the sleeve and one side seam. However, knitweave, with its low stitch count, is remarkably accommodating, and you will probably find the sleeve wide enough for most purposes.

2. You must plan and mark the needle bed beforehand. This particular design is so simple that you can work out the sleeve increases or decreases and shoulder shaping, if any, with a calculator and the Magic Formula (*see Chapter 9*). You will need to work out the number of stitches you require for the side seam and the sleeve top. If extra stitches are needed for the

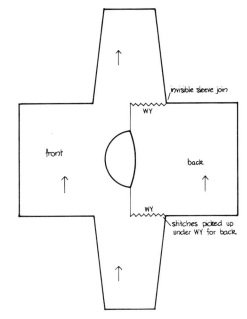

92 Option 3

shoulder seams, these are cast on after you have scrapped off in WY the back half of the first sleeve. Similarly, the extra stitches are cast off before you hang the waste swatch on the machine for the back half of the second sleeve. It is even easier to deal with these additional stitches on the second main piece.

The back half of the first sleeve is picked up for the back, and the side seam stitches cast on by the chain method or woven straight from a waste swatch. When you are weaving the first part, you must mark the needle which will be the one to receive the top of the shoulder stitch at the extreme left of the right half of the sleeve, when you come to weave the back. Mark the needles in repeats of 24 stitches across the bed. This sounds far more complicated than it really is. Take your diagram to the machine and you will see what it is all about.

You will, of course, note the row number on the punch or pattern card at the shoulder point where sleeve top joins the body piece. Roll the card to the appropriate number when you begin the back. Note that the shapings on the second sleeve are in reverse to the first, and decreases replace the increases. If you want a seamed side seam instead of a graft, then weave a few rows in pattern before you re-introduce the sleeve stitches. The pattern must, of course, be correct. At the far side, scrap off the stitches to be grafted to the back half of the second sleeve, and continue with a few rows of pattern on the side seam before casting or scrapping off. Apart from joining the top shoulder, underarm and side seams, we have only that one back shoulder seam to graft or stitch.

Option 4 (large based rolling repeats)

Our final option deals very effectively with the problems raised in the previous one. By this new method you can have a sideways knitwoven batwing with sleeves as wide as the needle bed will take. There are four pieces to knit: sleeve, front, sleeve, back.

Begin by knitting the right sleeve (full width). At the top, scrap off in WY and note the pattern row. Work out the needle arrangement for the front, then back, by seeing that the edge stitch at the shoulder co-ordinates with the centre sleeve pattern. Begin the front by using a cast on chain and by patterning from the next row

93 The invisible back shoulder joins

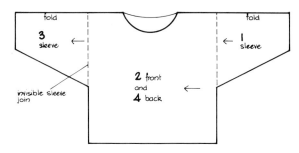

94 Option 4

following on from the sleeve top. At the far side, scrap off in WY and note the pattern row. Begin the second sleeve with a chain cast on and by following on in the pattern. The back, like the front, must also proceed from a chain at the pattern row following on from the first sleeve.

The secret to the seamless robe finish lies not only in matching the patterning needles exactly, but in the final putting together. On the back shoulder the cast on chain goes first on the needles, followed by the stitches below the WY.

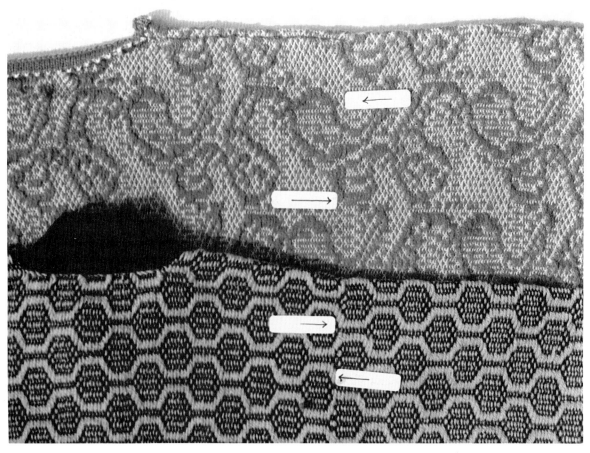

95 Lois Franklin. Horizontal striping in knitweave
(courtesy British Wool Marketing Board)

The chains are slipped over the stitches which are then cast off using the Fig. of 8 graft. Please note, the link-latch off method after an optimum tension row produces a sharp clean line, but not the desired effect of the seamless robe provided by the Fig. of 8.

If you wish to use the Option 4 technique on overall Fair Isle, you may find that the tight Japanese bind-off (see below) is just as good as the Fig. of 8. In fact, you could use the bind-off method on knitweave, but my preference is for the Fig. of 8. For one thing, it can be used to graft off loops that are too tight for any other method, unless of course one knits a loose row first. Try both techniques and make your choice. It is most unfortunate that machine knitting is dogged by authoritarian schools of thought and practice, and knitters are often reluctant to try methods other than those taught in colleges, clubs and classes, and indeed, in some well-loved publications. Incidentally, the reason for insisting that you cast on by the chain method is that it provides a pick-up loop which lies directly over the stitch, and that is why there can be a perfect alignment in a join with stitches below WY. With both the e wrap and the WY cast on method, the pick-up loops come between the stitches and not directly over them. This method provides us with an entirely new breakthrough in this area of garment design.

Necklines and a chain cast off

The second stitch on the first needle cast off produces a chain (to the back) similar to the link-latch off, but, unlike that, it is a controllable method. After you have placed the second stitch on the first needle (2 stitches on needle), you knit it off manually. Transfer it back to the empty needle and knit a new stitch with the yarn. The process is repeated all along the bed. This method is excellent to use in sideways knitting when you are casting off stitches for the front neck. You cast on again using a chain method. In this way both sides of the neck shaping can be matched successfully.

Sleeves

The use of stripes in sleeve design

Striping is a very effective way of patterning in sideways knitting and weaving. Indeed, self-coloured striping occurs automatically when we break the weave with stocking stitch rows or change the inlay yarn to another one. In coloured stripes there can be considerable variety. I usually, but not always, begin with a weaving yarn close in colour to the main yarn, and then stab the stripe alive with a little contrast inside its edges. Occasionally, I start with a contrast, and then lapse into the toning shade. It is difficult to lay down rules, as everyone's taste is different. My feeling is, however, that we must avoid looking like a deck chair at the seaside, and, if in doubt, go for the subtle rather than a too-bold stripe.

In this chapter, we confine ourselves to one problem relating to tops knitting, and that concerns the sleeve. I have noticed that when stripes appear in horizontal bands in a conventionally knitted top, then the same matching bands occur in the sleeve (*Fig. 95*). In other words, the arms as cylindrical limbs are clothed in the same pattern rhythm as the body, and my design sense tells me that this is right. If we apply the same principle to sideways knitting and straight sleeves, it means that since the stripes occur vertically on the trunk, they must surely occur vertically on the sleeve (*Fig. 91*). If that is so, then this means that seamless robe knitting with stripes cannot be applied in an elbow length or straight sleeve situation unless one alters the stripe proportions in some way (*Fig. 96*). More widely-spaced stripes are better than those closer together, especially for the arms. One can surely alter the proportions and still use the seamless robe method, by having a cape or bell-sleeve with stripes wide at first and then graduating in staggered intervals until the main striping sequence is reached at the ball of the shoulder.

A favourite approach is to stay with the seamless robe method for a cap-sleeved top or dress, but I would knit or weave full, elbow-length and long straight sleeves separately from the underarm seam upwards, and then have them fitted as well. Indeed, I did this instinctively for some time before I realised why I chose this method in preference to any other. Moreover, this approach leaves much more scope to introduce interesting weave patterns in the bodice, since the sleeves can be made to co-ordinate with the skirt.

1 Sample for Fig. 61

2 Patterns 1 and 2

3 Samples for Figs. 44, 85 and 128

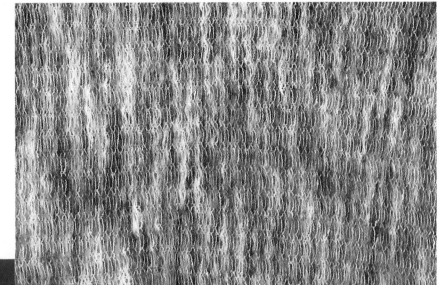

4 Fabric for Pattern 5

5 Pattern 5

6 Sample for Fig. 85

7 Pattern 7

8 Sample for Fig. 72

9 Samples for Figs. 78, 51, 66 and 37

10 Sample for Fig. 73

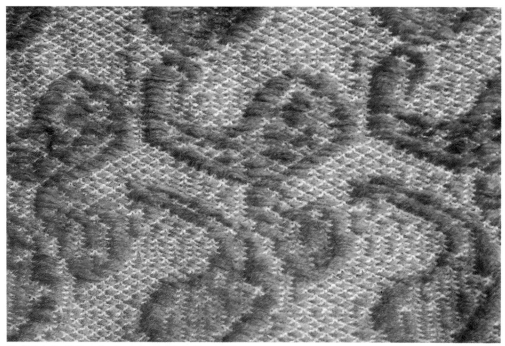

11 Fabric for Pattern 4 coloured with fabric dye pastels

12 Patterns 10 and 4

96 Lois Franklin 'Goya' pure wool and Italian mohair with viscose. Sideways knitwoven mermaid or tulip skirt. Note striping on sleeves (courtesy Knitting International)

97 Lois Franklin 'Cezanne' Italian space-dyed
mohair on pure wool with viscose and chenille. Note
striping on sleeve (courtesy Knitting International)

Droppage and the long sleeve

Some knitters complain that long sleeves drop during wear and after washing. Sleeves should not drop if the fabric is right and the arm has been measured correctly for length. Hold your arm relaxed by your side. Measure first from the ball of the shoulder to the wrist and then check by measuring from the centre back neck to the wrist. Take away the measurement for half of the back width. You are left with the ball of the shoulder to wrist measurement. Never measure for length with the arm outstretched. It is always about 5cm longer in this position and therefore gives a false measurement.

The seamless robe approach and cut and sew

These two methods are not as far apart as you first might think. With regard to stripes, the cut and sew knitter needs to work out their placement in the same way as the seamless robe knitter does. Moreover, all knitters knit the exact length required (front neck to bottom edge) widthways.

If I am using cut and sew, then I like to mark the critical shaping points with WY as guide marks to the scissors and the paper pattern which I use for cutting out. I allow 5mm for overlocking at the cut edges, and use the WY markers as guides in the stitching up also.

At most you need to cut out only the neck, armholes and sleeve heads. These can be overlocked so unobtrusively as to cause no more bulk than an ordinary seam. If the side seams are grafted and the bottom and top edges are selvages, who is to know that your garment is not the same as that produced by fully fashioned methods?

Note on marking the carriage slide rail

Marking with indelible pen the slide rail on which the carriage glides does no damage to the machine. As soon as you have finished the garment for which you have marked the bed, remove the pen marks with a cloth dipped in surgical spirit (untreated alcohol), then rub the rail with a lightly-oiled clean cloth. Many skirt knitters already use this method to mark flare sequences. Indeed, when you do flechage colour knitting, it is most helpful to mark the bed with different pens to show the colour change.

I mark the bed to indicate the salient patterning needle which must match the same patterning repeat needle at the joining point of the pieces in seamless robe knitting (i.e. top sleeve to back front shoulder). I do not know of a better way of solving the problem for all machines. Although some knitters recommend moving the needle strip to align 0 with the first needle left of centre, I feel this only adds to the confusion. Japanese punchcard designers, whether they are Brother, Knitmaster or Toyota, by no means adhere to the left needle pivot stitch principle. One only needs to study the hardbacked pattern books to see that. Quite often the designers choose the needle right of 0 on which to balance their 23 stitch designs. Some Brother needle strips (the older, thicker kind), have a habit of waltzing along under the needles anyway, and causing no end of bother when it comes to deciding which needle patterns what.

Perhaps the best reason of all for using the marking method is that it is an enormous help in sideways knitting when one is using a half size or half scale charter. Usually, the bottom half of a sideways knitted top (i.e. at the left) cannot be included on the charting sheet, so we mark the relevant needles on the left side of the bed to the point where the charter sheet begins (*Fig. 110*). I go further and mark the point where the armhole shaping stops and I cast on the large group of stitches up the yoke to the shoulder. I also enclose with marks the needles for the shoulder increase. These preparations speed up the knitting no end and ensure that the shaping is correct.

Since needle bed marking serves so many purposes, and is reasonably well known and practised, it is a good idea to stay with it as a general technique. So far I have not mentioned electronic knitters. They can choose where to place their patterns, although for this book it is best if they stay with the punchcard approach. It is worth pointing out that on the Brother 910, the dominant needle when the pattern selector is down is G1, which is the first needle right, not left of 0.

Waste yarn wedges (*Figs. 98 and 99*)

For jackets

I have been using this technique for some time on sideways knitting and have published information previously. The method has the advantage of holding fabric pieces together in a balanced tension until they are ready to be separated for making up or for the application of bands. Instead of beginning at the centre front of a jacket, begin as you would for a sweater at the side seam, so that the weave floats lie in the same direction all around the garment. Of course, if the pattern is designed for it, there is nothing to stop you weaving from the centre front outwards, or from the side seams outwards on the two jacket fronts.

To return to weaving the jacket front in one, when you get to the centre, lock the card or halt the pattern. You can organise it to stop at the correct point by starting at the appropriate pattern row. Work out the placement and number of rows beforehand. Change to stocking stitch, and knit one row with a ravel cord, then 12 rows of WY knitting, and one row with a

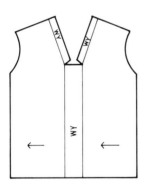

98 Waste yarn wedges in sideways knitted jackets

99 Waste yarn wedges in sideways knitted V-necked tops

100

second ravel cord (memorising-selecting row). Release the card and proceed with the weaving. If there is any shaping, as for a V, then it should be done by the HP method and scrapped off before the straight row WY wedge is begun on the first half of the front. For the second half, hang a waste swatch over the appropriate needles for the neck. Put the needles into HP and re-introduce them as required.

The next stage is to rib the first of the bands. When that is done, cut up the centre of the front leaving 6 rows of WY on each side. Pick up the MY stitches or bottom loops, pull out the ravel cord, and the WY piece falls away. Two stitches hang on one needle so slip one row over the other and bind off using your favourite method. Do the other band the same way. The method can be adapted to include facings as well as a band.

An alternative double stocking stitch band

This is an excellent choice for knitweave, conventionally or sideways knitted, as it offers a stable, sharply defined edging which does not easily flip over. You need to know the exact number of stitches to cast on over WY. After 6 rows of WY knit one row with a ravel cord. Change to MY and MT-1 (as for stocking stitch). Knit the depth of the band. If buttonholes are required, use the finished knitted-in method (see the pattern for the teenager's collared jacket).

On the fold, knit a loose row, MT+2, then the depth of hem at MT-1. Close the hem. Knit a row on MT. Pull out the ravel cord so that the WY falls away. With the wrong side facing, pick up centre front stitches. Knit one row on optimum tension, and link-latch off.

For V necked sweater tops

As knitters have observed, the V neck is liable to distortion when it is shaped in sideways knitwoven fabric. Apart from casting on and casting off in chains, there are two other methods you can use.

1. Hold the needles as the shaping proceeds on the first half and scrap off on to several rows of WY when the centre point of the V is reached. Immediately hang a waste swatch on the machine. Push the needles holding the waste swatch to HP, and re-introduce them in reverse to the shaping on the first half. This method is fairly easy. The disadvantage is that the V can still stretch out of shape, especially in fine

knitweave, although we can indeed chain the needles at the start of the edging.

2. Hold the needles as the shaping proceeds. At the centre point of the V remove the MY, lock or stop the pattern card and hold all needles left of the centre point of the V by taking them back to NWP, first on WY and then on a ravel cord. Better still, use the garter bar. Take the carriage to the right. Using WY and the HP intarsia method, re-introduce the needles in the same row and stitch sequence in which they were held, until the centre point of the V is reached.

From the centre outwards, push the same shaping sequences to HP as you knit until the wedge is complete and all needles are in HP. Leave them like this and break off the WY. Bring the needles at the left, held at NWP, back into WP. With carriage on slip-part-empty, memorise-select the pattern.

Insert MY, release card and proceed. This time, you will see precisely where you re-introduce the needles for the second part of the V shaping. When it is complete at the top of the shoulder-neck base, you will find that both sides of the neck are being held at equal tension by the WY intarsia wedge. If you draw the whole thing on your charting device sheet, you will be able to visualise the method, but will need to work out the HP sequences for every alternate row.

Remember, you take the carriage to the right to start the WY wedge, and you knit in stocking stitch a right-angled triangle to the halfway mark. The second part is also a right-angled triangle, the two together making an isosceles triangle with two equal long sides (*Fig. 100*). This wedge shape is used in skirt knitting for a full flare and this particular exercise is a most useful introduction to the principle of flechage knitweave on tops.

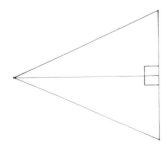

100 The two right-angled triangles in a flare

At the end of the weaving, cut down the centre of the WY wedge to the point of the V. When you come to apply a band or edging, you will be able to pick up the stitches and knit the edging directly from the V neck edge. Because you did not wrap the HP needles during the knitting and shaping of the WY intarsia wedge, you will have a row of decorative holes like a diagonal on an all-in-one raglan.

Method notes

The NWP method of holding needles

When we hold for any length of time needles on a fabric which is to be knit side right side, there are no problems whether we choose the HP or NWP ravel cord method. However, when we are knitting a purl side right side fabric like knitweave, we can have the problem of rubbed up stitches and floats which can make a bad mark across the garment. The NWP method is nevertheless better than the HP one in this situation, but one must first knit the stitches manually with a piece of waste yarn, then knit them back to NWP with the ravel cord. In this way, the MY stitches will have dropped below the reach of the wheels and brushes that cause the damage in the first place.

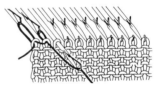

101 Taking stitches back to NWP

An even better way is to take the stitches to be held onto a piece of the garter bar. First, hang the three-pronged tool onto the WP needles immediately to the right or left of the stitches to be taken off so that the garter bar will not drag the edge stitches from the needles. When you have removed the stitches onto the garter bar and pushed them well down on the prongs, drop the garter bar into the gate peg recess immediately below the needles to which the held stitches must be returned. The garter bar can rest there out of reach of the underside of the carriage and its wheels and brushes.

The use of darts

The method by which one has to knit bust darts in sideways knitting is such a clumsy one that it is best forgotten. A good and easy way is to shave off a right-angled triangular wedge at each bottom corner by increasing to the full complement and then at the far side decreasing the appropriate amount. Alternatively, we can shape by the HP method. By chipping off each corner, we prevent the edges from dropping and compensate for any pull-up that can occur in the middle from V neck shaping. I find that I need to widen the bottom of a long sideways knitted jacket and I do this by knitweaving two narrow flares at the back lower edge and one on each of the fronts. Long sleeves knitted sideways can also be shaped by the HP method.

The invisible seam, held stitches and a fashioned edge

If we understand how the fabric behaves when we put the pieces together (and we have already discussed pattern matching), then we should know what technique to use in the final making up. If we do not have a vocabulary of techniques, then we must resort to all kinds of complicated ways round problems. Perfection may be our objective, but the knitting and making up must be achieved easily and within reasonable time. If a process is too complicated it should be abandoned, for surely there is a better way. Moreover, knitters with limited time to spare will not attempt it anyway.

No fabric taxes our ingenuity more than seamless robe fabric knitwoven sideways. Not only are there sometimes limitations on the kind of surface pattern we can choose, but the above and below floats, together with the bottom loops and stitches, create making-up problems as bad as those created for the dressmaker by pile velvet. Having said that, I must admit that the results can be so pleasing that efforts to master the problems are well worth while.

Essentially the same list of making-up and knitting techniques appears in every manual. With very few exceptions (*Silver-Knitmaster's Guide to Knitting Techniques* being one) the manuals' concern is with making-up techniques when the knit side of the fabric is the right side. To cope with knitweave in every situation, we need to extend our vocabulary of techniques and include others not so well known but which are

ideal for this new situation. I have already discussed various methods of casting on and off. Here are two more you may find useful.

1. The weaving cast on method. I have been experimenting with this method, using the weft yarn to lay across the WP needles on the first row (1x1 selection). I have had considerable success in making a perfect match in the final seam. The weaving cast on, like the chain, provides you with actual stitches to pick up and this is the reason for the success. The technique provides the quickest way to cast on, but its drawback is instability.

2. The tight Japanese bind-off (*Fig. 102*). This method is probably easier to learn and quicker to do than the Fig. of 8 graft. The bind-off technique provides nearly as good a seaming method as the Fig. of 8. Its finish is flat and smooth and it is good to use in the application of single thickness ribbed bands.

102 The Japanese bind-off

Quite a few manuals illustrate the technique, but they usually instruct the knitter to knit one row optimum tension, after one lot of stitches has been slipped over the other. The bind-off takes place through the final row. I find this method too slack, and the seam gapes in knitweave as badly as it does when the link-latch off is used. Instead, slip one row of stitches over the other. For ease, see that both lots of stitches are knitted at MT+1 before the WY knitting. Now bind-off immediately and tightly, doing your stem stitches through the last row of stitches hanging on the needles. As you bind off, rip off the secured stitches from the needles to get your fingers behind to hold and pull down the fabric, thereby opening the stitches for the tapestry needle to go through. I have used this method with a 2/24s bright acrylic as base yarn, and a 4-ply acrylic as weft. On the right side, the fabric – a 1x1 ORR pattern – matched perfectly. The seam only gaped a little when I pulled really hard on each side of the fabric. If necessary, the sides of the seam can be invisibly slip stitched together, but often you can tighten the last knitting rows by pulling the yarn through manually to tighten the final join.

Additional uses of the Fig. of 8

1. The Fig. of 8 is excellent to use as a seaming method on ribbed welts. These can be very difficult to seam neatly, as many photographs of pattern garments reveal only too clearly. It is important to allow one extra stitch, at the left usually, of each welt, so that stitches one and two are on the same bed (main or ribber).

2. Though a row on optimum tension and the link-latch off method provide a quicker way, I often prefer to use the Fig. of 8 in a situation like the application of ribbed bands to jacket fronts, where the reverse side is shown nearly as often as the right, and where the suppleness of the graft ensures that the band lies correctly. The wrong side of the graft has an attractive, crochet-like appearance and it has no bulk like mattress stitch. It has one main disadvantage: if the graft is not done tightly then the seam can gape a little. This is, however, easy to draw together for a perfect match. The more I use the graft, the more I wish to commend it as the most versatile and beautiful of any seaming method in our craft.

Incidentally, one method we cannot use on overall knitweave is the stocking stitch graft (Kitchener stitch, USA). It creates one bald stocking stitch row in the middle of fabric with weave floats. I do, however, use the stocking stitch graft occasionally on skirts with knitweave sections, providing the base yarn is not too fine.

The sewing machine and professional linker

The sewing machine makes a clean, sharp line down a seam, and if you are not going to use seamless robe methods, then you will get the best results by:

1. Casting on and casting off, using chain methods preferably, so that both edges are the same. Cast on after a few rows of WY. You can also use the e wrap.

2. Knitting the sleeve separately. Match the pattern direction by using the reverse weave for the second sleeve.

3. Using a binding wire, from Brother dealers, to wind in and out of the chain stitches at the fabric edges. The seam will be straight and firm

for stitching. See that you have no weave floats trapped between the edges before you stitch.

4. Choosing a medium straight stitch. If you use a stretch stitch be sure your seam is correct before you start. Stretch stitches are notoriously difficult to unpick.

Professional linkers also do a very good job on knitweave. Knit one row before the WY rows without weaving to make linking easier. If you want to use the Knitmaster or Brother linker, hitch your two pieces back on the machine, right sides together, pushing the needles through below the cast on and cast off chains. Knit a row on T10 and link off. In some cases, you may have to knit the final loose row by hand. If you stitch by hand, then you must use a small, firm back stitch, and a double strand of base yarn, or a suitable smooth yarn which matches in colour.

The steaming, pressing method

There is a strong case for pinning out and blocking where knitweave tops, skirts and dresses are concerned. You need an iron with plenty of steam. Try your tension piece first. Steam and gently press. Do not be heavy-handed with the textured weaves in particular – you could destroy the appeal. I like to have a towel and a blanket on the ironing board underneath the cover so that the steam will go through. The springy surface provided by the undercovers absorbs the steam, supports the weave and prevents the pattern from getting flattened by the iron. In fine knitweave, however, we do need more pressure on the iron because we de-bulk for drape. The weft holds the fabric firmly and prevents an overkill even if the yarn is synthetic.

When you have tried out your pressing method, pin out each garment piece to size. Steam and press in the same way as you practised on your swatch (see next chapter). Leave to cool and dry and then unpin. Let the pieces relax a little before making up by the method of your choice.

Laundering knitweave

Gently handwash. After rinsing, spin the garment in a pillowcase to restrict movement. Pull it into shape and dry flat. Sideways knitwoven garments are less trouble than the conventionally knitted ones, which can drop long and thin, so treat these with the greatest care of all.

Welts and bottom edges

Consider carefully what welt or band will look best on your top to co-ordinate with the skirt. If you are sideways knitweaving, then you must add the welt afterwards and use a flexible joining method. If you prefer the optimum tension row and the link-latch off method, you can press the ribber into service to loosen the last row even more. Put 1 in 4 needles into WP on the ribber. Knit the optimum tension row with the ribber on H5. Release loops off ribber needles and cast off. Because we use predominantly soft-spun synthetic yarns, welts in the same yarns are in danger of having no grip. Incorporate transparent nylon thread or fine thread elastic in the welts. Here are some choices to think about before we discuss the skirts.

1. Rib or mock welts are good to use at the bottom edge of dolmans and jackets, especially where there is a blouson effect above. In fact, a good case can be made for using the mock welt in preference to the single rib. The former provides just the right amount of firmness and weight to match the main knitweave fabric.

2. Hems are a favourite choice, often drawn in with a rouleau or cord, on or just below the hipline. These make a top pleasing to look at and very easy to wear. They can make match-mates look like a single piece outfit without an apparent break.

3. Peplums are also very flattering. They can be in rib, or lightly gathered to the bottom edge.

4. Tabard side slits are not as popular as they deserve to be. They can be edged with braid. The fabric falls slim and straight over the hipline with no grip at all. Wear with a rouleau slotted through the fabric at the waist.

5. Mohair jackets, sideways knitwoven, and knitted on a lacy setting, can present problems. A rib welt can militate against the bands of the front opening. If you just turn up a hem, the fabric flops and waves. My preference is for a deliberately styled blouson effect, with the bottom edge drawn in by welt or rouleau and front bands that co-ordinate with the effect at the bottom edge.

Pockets

Pockets in knitweave need careful planning beforehand. They can be patch, single- or double-lined, or pouch. The easiest pocket to knit is the placket pocket. A gap is left in the side seam and a stocking stitch pouch is inserted either by picking up the edge loops, graft knitting from those or by stitching on afterwards. The technique employed for knitted-in pockets depends on whether you knitweave sideways or in the conventional way and whether you want a horizontal or vertical slit. Tip: when you want to mark a pocket placement, thread a needle with a strand of contrasting weft, and weave over the area you want marked.

Horizontal slit for a lined pocket

In a conventional knitwoven garment, take off the selected stitches onto a piece of WY. Tie and leave. Hitch on the stitches from a pre-knitted lining and continue. On completion of the piece, the pocket top is ribbed or knitted from the stitches left on WY. In sideways knitwoven fabric you have to create a vertical slit for it to appear horizontal in wearing. The pattern row is noted. Stitches are held while first one side and then the other side is knitted. The pouch and pocket top are added afterwards.

Vertical slit for a double pouch lining

The methods are the same as above but in reverse, depending on whether you knit sideways or conventionally. Study the method employed for the knitting of the pouch onto a vertical slit in the pattern for the child's hooded jacket. Please note: you can attach a separate pouch to a horizontal slit created by the WY buttonhole method.

Patch pockets

It is very difficult to surface-sew neatly the edges of a separately knitwoven patch into position on a garment piece. Turn the garment piece on its side, right side facing, and poke through the needles. Hang the edge loops of one side of the patch, right side facing, onto the needle hooks. Close the latches and pull through to the other side. Knit a row on the optimum tension and link-latch off or use the

Fig. of 8 graft. Do the other two sides the same. This gives a knitted-in, neat effect.

Warning: regard knitwoven pockets as mainly a design accessory with an ornamental use. A pocket can hold a handkerchief, but never a bunch of keys. You can line pockets, but it is so easy to make them look too stiff, though you can stabilise with a soft synthetic interlining. The best way is to treat pockets with respect and make them as perfectly as possible.

A *final thought*

Fabric knitwoven conventionally, from bottom edge to neck, can be treated in the same way as any other fabric from the knitting machine. Apart from laundering there are nowhere near the same number of problems to challenge us as there are in sideways knitwoven fabric; but in choosing the easy option every time, we are missing the most versatile and interesting aspects of knitweave. Certainly, we would never experience the fluidity and the drape that this fabric can achieve.

8 Sideways knitted and knitwoven skirts

In the UK the interest in sideways knitting continues unabated. The style is free and flowing and is the antithesis of the classic, trim narrow lines of the Chanel suit. The knitted skirt is frowned upon by a media dominated by handknit values. On the other hand, machine knitters regard the fashion industry with growing exasperation for seeming to be forever stuck with heavy knitted tops. Not only does the industry neglect the many women who are size 14 and over, but it also ignores those of any size who choose elegance as their guiding principle.

In this chapter, I am emphasising the separate skirt more than the dress. Nevertheless, the dress can be as flattering on a mature figure, especially if the garment is sideways knitted and incorporates areas of colour and pattern which emphasise slimming lines. If you want a dress, as distinct from a skirt, you will need your back neck to waist measurement plus 2.5-4cm for lengthwise ease, or for blouson effect. When the skirt and top are joined together, preferably on the knitting machine, you should continue knitting a casing for the elastic, i.e. a double hem attached to the waistline. An alternative is to make a row of holes and slot a cord or rouleau through at the waist. No knitted dress should be without support at the waist, as without this it will drop. You should knit or weave a belt, or buy one to match the dress. A ribbed cummerbund joined to top and skirt is another attractive possibility.

Though there is growing interest in sideways knitwoven skirts, at the time of writing we have seen very few pattern translations into total knitweave of the skirt shapes we like to wear in the UK, and which are so popular in other stitch patterns.

The principle

The Japanese, who may not do as much total look sideways knitting as we do, at least have shown us how to work out mathematically the angle of flare in a sideways knitted skirt, which is based on the segment of a circle. This has proved a most versatile prototype from which to develop variations from a nearly straight A-line to a very full circular skirt. Currently, the favourite skirt is a medium circular, with a soft pleated one, a gentle A-line in shape, running it a close second. Either of these skirts makes a good matchmate for tops with full sleeves in fashion at the moment.

Definition

This is a skirt which is composed of flares and straight row wedges. The latter come together at the waist line to form the waist line measurement, plus 5-10cm ease, sometimes more or sometimes less. The hip measurement requires the addition of 5-7cm ease for a moderate A-line shape. The flares give the additional measurement to the bottom hem but they are not included in the waist measurement plus ease. You can have half flares or full flares. We concentrate on the latter here, though the principle is the same for both.

Flares are achieved by short-rowing and holding position. An allover knitwoven skirt takes longer to do than the stocking stitch version with weaving sections. A full flare is known as a flechage (arrow-shaped) in the industry and is composed of an even number of rows divisible by four; but the complement is 4 rows less than you would imagine, so five flaring groups produce 16, not 20 rows, because the flaring takes place every alternate row at the waist side in a 2 row sequence. Each of the numbers in the diagram (*Fig. 103*) represents 2

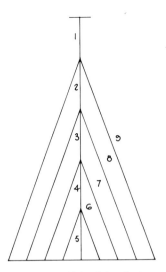

103 The flaring pyramid in skirt design

rows. That means that the carriage ought to travel along the same group of WP needles four times: 2 rows to put the HP needles at the left to hold and 2 rows to return them to the WP group. There are two exceptions to the rule. One is the centre group, no. 5, and the other is the last group, no. 9. The carriage passes over these two groups of WP needles only twice. No. 9 group is of course the first group. When you push it finally back into UWP, all the needles are ready to knit the straight row wedge. The next 2 rows begin the wedge and are not counted as the last 2 rows of the flare.

The flare

Deciding on the flare

There are two main decisions to take.

1. We must decide on the width of the bottom hem in proportion to the waist plus ease. We must also take the length into consideration. The following applies to A-line and gentle roll-pleat skirts. When a skirt is pleated at the waist line, the waist to hemline ratios are less important than the pleat formation one wishes to achieve. On the popular A-line variations the ratio of waist to bottom hem could be approximately, or exactly, 2:3, 3:4, 3:5, 1:2, 1:3 and so on.

2. We must decide on the number of straight row wedges that come together at the waistline. The narrower the wedge, the more there will be (*Fig. 91*). The fewer the number, the wider they

are, and the wider the flare will be in a moderate A-line (see next chapter). On narrow skirts, with a definite roll pleat formation, the flaring should be between two and four times, and no more. Otherwise the pleat will be thrown out of line. Therefore, the straight row wedge will be narrow also, since the flechage is composed of its width plus the correct proportion to produce the ratio. Most knitters cannot visualise the proportions of the skirt they want to knit. They choose a pattern in the hope that it will fit. If we understand a few of the principles, then perhaps we can choose with greater wisdom and eventually move on to designing our own.

I began designing skirts with a 10 panel base on a 1:2 ratio which produces in my length a gentle, moderate A-line. I then moved on to 15, 20 and 25 panels. The information and experience gained in stocking stitch and knitweave sections transferred easily to the total knitweave situation, though this situation, as we shall see, has its own problems and areas of special design interest.

The angle of flare exercise

This is a diagrammatic method used by the Japanese which I have adapted to design circular skirts. In *A Resource Book Pattern Supplement* I discussed the method in a very basic way, and used it to analyse my 10 panel prototype skirt. I have continued to experiment and here are some of my latest findings. You will discover, as I have done, that the exercise is an extremely valuable one, and it is well worth taking a pencil, paper, ruler and a pair of compasses to try it.

The exercise is valuable for two reasons. It provides you with a visual image of the shape of the skirt. (We tend to forget how the length of the skirt affects its proportions.) It also allows for the crucial importance of the hipline. If you mark the hipline at the exact point at which it comes below the waist, 18-20cm, you can tell by measuring the line whether the skirt is just right for you at the widest point. You will be able to tell if you need to adjust the groups of flaring needles to provide more or less ease. Here we try the exercise to scale, but you can draw the skirt full size on a large piece of paper (newspaper will do), using your measurements, a soft felt pen, a ruler and a piece of string with pencil at one end and drawing pin at the other to act as a pair of compasses.

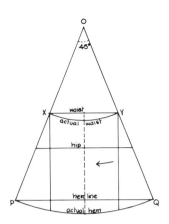

104 The angle of flare exercise

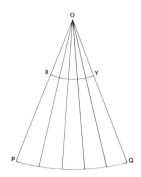

105 Segmented skirt

To try the exercise, on a piece of A4 paper, nearer the bottom than the top, draw a rectangle 10 x 15cm, the short side at the bottom. Put a line for the hip about 3-4cm down from x and v (*Fig. 104*). At the bottom hem edge, extend the lines at each side by 5cm (p and q). The extension is, of course, half your waistline of 10cm. The hemline (p-q) is now double the waist (x-y), and you have a mini-prototype skirt in the ratio 1:2. Extend the hipline on both sides. In the real situation you would check this for size and ease (5-7cm average).

From the extremities of the extended hemline take the diagonals, px and pq, to each end of the waistline, and continue them until they meet at the angle of flare, 0, which in this skirt length and ratio of 1:2 is around 45 degrees. Put your compasses at the centre of 0, and using one of the diagonals as a radius, draw the curves at waist and hemline. These will provide you not so much with lines for measuring, but with a drawing of the three-dimensional shape, xyqp, which fits the cylindrical shape of the human body. You have to ask yourself as you study it: 'Is this the shape I am aiming for?' If it is not then you must change the proportions at the hemline, bearing in mind that yarn choice could affect the shape as well. If you want the hemline narrower, try a third at each side; if wider, add a quarter to your half, making three quarters, and so on. Remember that you are looking at only half the shape widthways, but though we shall see only 5 segments instead of 10, the ratios are correct (*Fig. 105*). Moreover, in the real situation you would at least see the length of skirt you need and its relationship to the shape you have drawn. Please note, the length

will alter the angle of flare. You cannot consider width proportions without reference to length. Both width and length factors affect flare breakdowns.

Since in our example the angle of flare is approx. 45 degrees, each of those segments cuts an angle of 9 degrees. Draw the lines as accurately as you can. At the bottom, you can join them above the arc, and you will find near enough that the measurement is double that of each one at the waistline. The measurement of the one at the hemline is composed of the flare and the straight row wedge. What is most important is that this particular circle segment skirt depends on equal and balanced flaring along the whole length in order to achieve its shape. We use the Magic Formula and the methods described in the next chapter to work it out.

Very few of us have perfect figures, and it is at this point that we start to alter and refine the shape for other skirt types we would like to wear. If we have a pencil-slim figure, are using fine knitweave and want the flaring to stop at the thighs, so that the folds can fall soft and straight, then we would set about organising the flaring groups differently. There are variations too which allow us to flare only two or three times along the bed, because we want a very full pleated skirt in thick and thin effects.

The flare and the wedge

The great value of using this 10 sectioned skirt as an example is that we can easily divide our waist plus ease by 10. We multiply by the number of rows for 1cm (from our tension swatch) to find the rows and then divide the answer by 10. Twice that number goes into the flare exactly or approximately. Supposing the flare figure is divisible by 2 and not by 4, how do we overcome this problem? We may decide we can do without those extra two rows; if we do want them, however, then we take two from each of the straight row wedges and sandwich these extra rows in the centre of the flare. This means that in an overall weave all needles are tooled back into WP and we weave the two rows. Then we repeat the same half flare again before completing the rest of the wedge.

If we use this method, we need to have around 20 sections and not 10. The wedge and half flare formation have to be narrow and the skirt knitted in soft yarn to prevent a lop-sided swing. One of the most successful skirts I have ever produced was knitted in this way (25 complete sections in a fine bouclé, with knitweave straight row wedges).

You can also divide the flare into two equal parts with 2 weaving rows separating the mirrored halves. Another way is to separate the half flares with equal proportions of straight rows. In fact there are many permutations on the theme. However, when you use half flares always be aware of the possibility of too much swing to one side, and so keep the flare count low, and the sections small and numerous.

It is important to organise the one complete section at the waistline as a manageable unit. If it is too large, you may have to re-organise the whole series, because the skirt must match at the join, and half a section that is a mismatch will not do. This is why it is a good idea to have in your mind at the onset the number of sections that you want, even though your 10 may become 11, and your 15, 17 and so on. This is a decision you take towards the end of your knitting when you can assess the fabric you are producing much more accurately. For the knitting of dresses, of course, the calculation must be much more precise. As a general rule and for the basic skirt knitting that we do mostly, there are no hard and fast rules, only guidelines.

1. Does the skirt fit?
2. Is it suitable for what you have in mind?
3. Does it look and feel good?
4. Does it wash and launder well?
5. Does it keep its shape?

One certainty is that the 10 section prototype and its variations appear to suit a surprising number of people, so maybe the circle segment is the norm after all.

The total look

It is necessary to consider whether your skirt is the right co-ordinate for the top you are going to wear. Moreover, it is rather important that the top does not have to cover too many folds of skirt from waist to hip, so in your calculations consider what the total look impact will be. Do remember nothing alters the impact of a skirt shape more than a batwing (*Fig. 109*).

The flare principle and knitweave sections

We flare with the carriage at the right side, hem side, and push out to hold the needles at the left side, waist side, only when the carriage is at the right, i.e. every alternate row. In stocking stitch flares, we wrap the edge HP needle or else push another out to prevent a hole as the carriage moves back to the right. The needle groups are returned similarly. In this situation, the weaving section begins at and continues from the right, and in any colour change the yarn will be looped at the right edge. We can only really use a hem at the bottom in order to hide the yarn stranded up the edge.

When we come to knit a skirt with stocking stitch flares and weaving wedges, we can organise the weaving to begin at the left. There will be at least 2 rows of stocking stitch to be included in the measurement of the straight row wedge. We will knit a memorising-selecting row from right to left to start the weave, and at the end of it, there will be another row, from left to right, to take us to the beginning of the flare. If we wish the flare to be centrally placed, then we can have 2, 6, 10 stocking stitch straight rows, i.e. odd numbers when divided by two, because we are changing our starting and finishing points from left to right.

Counting the sections

The use and non-use of the row counter
(tip from Denise Musk)
Since the straight row wedges make up the waist, only the row count which relates to those is of significance. To avoid confusion and to make for an easy check method, disconnect the row counter at the beginning of the flare and connect it again when the flare is complete.

Using waste yarn as a tally
Have a spare cone of marker yarn beneath the machine at the right-hand side. When each

complete section is knitted, lift up the marker yarn and lay it over the end needle. Loops are formed for easy counting and each loop represents a complete section.

Knitweave in skirts

There are two approaches to this type of knitting, explained in detail below.

Stocking stitch flares and weaving straight row wedges

In the UK, patterning straight row wedges is a very popular way of incorporating weave. For one thing this skirt type is so easy and quick to do. While the patterned weave wedges are knitted straight, the stocking stitch flares are shaped in no time at all. The patterned weave creates gentle rolled pleats which are very attractive. We do, of course, always get a striped pattern using this technique, but the variety can be considerable. It is important to choose a base yarn that has good draping qualities in stocking stitch.

Total knitweave

There is growing interest in this type of skirt knitting, partly because of the considerable space devoted to it in South African publications, and partly because of the distinctive appeal of its fabric. The machine knitting world owes Audrey Palmer a debt of gratitude for exploring the superb working relationship of 2/24s bright acrylic as base, and soft 'forgiving' yarns as weft. For those who are beginning to tire of the ubiquitous Fair Isles and intarsias, fluid knitweave offers a unique and beautiful alternative. Many home knitters whose time is at a premium find the amount of work involved in total knitweave rather daunting, though no one has commented on how long it takes to do lace panels. It is not surprising, therefore, that only a handful of our top designers, whose garments command high prices, find the total knitweave approach a commercial proposition.

Problems and some possible remedies

Here are a few suggestions for coping with the problems discovered in the knitting of total or overall weave skirts. I hope more of us are inspired to enter into this fascinating and highly rewarding area of the craft.

The turning scars

The key problem, as I see it, is the ugly mark left by the wrapping yarns, base and weft, round the turning post needles of the HP group. Incidentally, do check that any fitted tuck brushes are inoperative before you start. Even if we employ a self-wrapping method, the brushes and wheels rub up the yarns, especially in a situation where we flare more than five or six times. It is the yarn wraps nearest the waist side which are the casualties, as they take the greatest punishment from the underside wheels and brushes which pass them and rub them more times proportionately than they do those nearest to the hem edge. We can understand why knitweavers of skirts choose soft, fluffy and/or textured yarns in order to hide the turning scars. Here are some possible solutions.

1. We hang waste knitting all along the sinker pins as a protection. This method I reject totally as a clumsy, slow procedure. If we are reduced to this we might as well stay with stocking stitch.

2. We do not flare lower than the thighs. The marks are thus concentrated nearer to the waist and we can hide the worst of them with a sweater or top. Moreover we do not flare more than five times. The disadvantage is the restriction these two precautions place on the skirt styles we may choose.

3. To minimise the turning scars, you can employ the following self-wrapping method (see the next chapter for another).

First mark the flaring groups on the bed with an indelible marker. Push out to HP the needle group up to the first mark. Knitweave to the left. Push the last WP needle into hold. Do not wrap that needle with the weaving yarn. Knitweave to the right. The needle has wrapped itself and you have speeded up the process.

In the second half of the flare, you must tool back one extra needle immediately to the left of each mark on the bed. Then push it out to HP for the return to the right, following the procedure above. It doesn't matter in the least that two adjacent needles instead of one are wrapped in the two halves of the flare, providing the same two are chosen. They are wrapped only once, and are on the left and right of the indelible marks. Try a sample and choose quite deliberately a smooth crisp yarn as weft. You will see that the mark at the extreme right, bottom hem edge of your swatch is hardly visible. What is more, you can ease back some of the more obvious floats into the weave fabric.

4. We can take the eyes away from any marks there are by introducing colour, and other stitch patterns and effects in the straight row wedges. If we are adventurous we might try patterning the flares.

5. When we flare more than six or seven times we should divide the flare into two halves. If we flare, say, nine times, then we complete the first half. The needles must be tooled back into B position (Knitmaster), or into their patterning positions B and D (Brother and Toyota). Remember that any straight knitweave rows over the full complement of needles in the middle of the flare are counted in the wedge. We continue to complete the second half of the flare. By adopting this procedure, we are preventing the wheels and brushes from savaging the same area of weave in the second half of the flare, and we can have any skirt shape of our choice based on the circle segment.

The manual selection of needles
The knitter has to tool back the needle groups in the second half of the flare. For speed I use the seven-eyed adjustable tool, all prongs out, for Knitmaster, and selected in pattern for Brother and Toyota (1x1). First, with your fingers, push the needle group to UWP, stitches behind latches, latch tips touching the sinker pins. The selected needles on the Brother and Toyota can stay in this position. Now use the tool. A three-eyed tool also works well on the Knitmaster. I find I can complete this process very speedily, and really I am only minimally slower than I would be working in stocking stitch. It does mean, however, that we will choose the basic, easy to select ORR weave at least for the flares. These patterns do, after all, produce the best drape and we can liven them up in various ways. If we do not select manually in the tooling back process, streaks of stocking stitch will ruin the weave. The flare must be in pattern.

The use of two knitweave patterns in a skirt
The value of understanding the flare process and how many rows you will achieve by the flare count is appreciated when you come to punch a combined card of two patterns, one for the straight row wedge and one for the flare. Begin by trying card 1, using a rolling repeat for a straight row wedge and card 1 locked (ORR) for the flare. Then try punching the basic diagonal

or a mini-chevron for the straight row wedge and the 1x1 ORR repeat for the flare (*Fig. 18*). Count your rows carefully and check before you punch. Electronic knitters will, of course, find this procedure very quick and easy to do.

Note on unpressed pleating in knitweave: the unpressed pleat is created by knitting methods and is therefore permanent. The underpleats in the Hobby two-piece (see garment pattern section) have to be steam pressed into place after washing and drying. The weave section is stitched down on one side by the sewing machine to create an outer ridge. All the pleats flow in one direction like a knife-pleated fabric skirt. It is a good idea to do a sample piece of one complete section in the pattern of your choice to check that the pleat or fold hangs correctly. Soft folds often form automatically as a result of the methods employed in the flare and straight row wedges. Other pleat structures are created in the knitting from an outer fold marked by a thicker ridge, and an inner fold marked by a narrow ditch created by a thinner section.

There are various ways of creating the thick and thin areas in knitweave. Be prepared to experiment first to test the effect you have in mind. Different yarn combinations react in different ways and you can come up with some surprises, usually pleasant ones.

The ORR basic weave: thick and thin, ridge and hollow

Please note the following points.

1. Because knitweave is usually a purl side right side fabric, some of the following effects will be reversed on a knit side right side fabric.

2. In 1 to 4 below, the stitch patterns advocated – weave, slip, tuck, Fair Isle and thread lace – are all from the same 1x1 ORR repeat. You merely switch from the weave to the stitch of your choice and back again. Since knitweave is basically stocking stitch, the tuck loops and slip stitches are knitted off straight away.

3. You can achieve up to 2 pattern rows in partial knitting with no other precaution than by pushing the needles not required to HP (wrap the needle). This technique can be employed at the hem edge of a skirt as well as on a top, and you can use two or three pairs of partial pattern rows in a group.

106 Skirt sample showing the use of reversed FI and slip stitch in the pleat formation

Techniques which provide contrast

1. You can knit instead of knitweaving the inlay yarn or suitable alternative for a ridge and leave 2 rows unwoven with just the base yarn knitting. The latter creates a hollow.

2. Two to 4 rows reverse Fair Isle after 2 rows of base yarn knitted solo, makes a ridge above a hollow. You can use the weaving yarn (two ends) for Fair Isle, and/or a colour contrast yarn if you wish. The surface looks like ridged top stitching. Another top stitch effect is achieved by using thread lace (Knitmaster) with the main yarn as the lace thread.

3. Tuck stitch after stocking stitch, and on the edge of a weave section, makes a ridge. In the middle of a weave it makes a hollow.

4. A hollow is created by changing to 2 rows knit, 2 rows slip stitch, or to a lace eyelet pattern. 4 rows slip, on the other hand, makes a good sharp edge for a knife pleat.

107 Lois Franklin 'Giotto' space-dyed Italian mohair with pure wool. Note coloured intarsia wedges (courtesy Knitting International)

108 Lois Franklin dress in total knitweave with
curved intarsia flechage (courtesy Lois Franklin
Designer Knitwear)

5. We can pleat by tension change, tight for a ridge, loose for a hollow. Rounded roll pleats also form when we change to two ends of base yarn instead of one. As soon as we remove one of the ends we create an inner pleat.

The use of colour with pattern

If you want to try intarsia knitweave, then it is simple to have one colour for the flare and a second for the straight row wedge. Any other variations should be planned first and tried. When you want a top to co-ordinate then draw the insertion on the garment block, and work out the HP sequences by means of the Magic Formula.

Colour change in the base yarn

I am only just beginning to experiment with this but I am delighted with the results so far. In fact, the approach is the easiest way to introduce clearly defined shapes of colour contrast which can be as subtle or as dramatic as you choose. For one thing, you do not have to worry about merging the contrast weave to a point in the flechage, because you stay with the same weaving yarn, which will be altered in hue by the contrast underneath. If you use more than one colour contrast then you will require another tension mast. Remember that the 4-way mast for the double bed colour changer has powerfully tensioned wires. If you are going to change colour, then use the 4-way mast for both the tension swatch and the garment. You may find that you have to alter the number on the stitch dial by up to one whole number looser.

Skirt styles in sideways knitted total knitweave

Sometimes it is recommended that we employ a few plain knitting rows in a straight row wedge to hide the join, if nothing else. This means that we immediately create a stripe effect which could have an inhibiting influence on the top we wish to make. There is nothing to stop us from weaving the skirt in two parts with joins at the side seam. If we do this, then we can still weave the skirt in one piece, but we separate the sections halfway with 12 to 14 rows of WY, followed by a chain cast on to begin the second piece as we began the first.

At the end, scrap off in WY. Cut the WY joining section in half. Hitch the MY chains onto the needles first, followed by the stitches (right sides together). Slip the one lot over the other and use the Fig. of 8 graft or the Japanese bind-off. Remove WY.

In a stocking stitch skirt with weaving sections, we can either graft the seam (Kitchener stitch, USA), or place the join right against a weaving section so that it is hidden, and use a quick link off. Because of the methods of casting on and casting off I employ, I find no skirt style in sideways knitted total knitweave is barred to me. I would, of course, choose the yarn with care and avoid a too smooth weft, though the dress in Patsy Amanda is remarkably successful, and the join in the back skirt is only a faint shadow with the weft loops perfectly aligned. There, as always, I used a chain cast on and the Fig. of 8 graft in the final join.

Dealing with the hem edge (total knitweave)

When you are knitweaving a summer-weight skirt, please see that the weaving yarn is caught in firmly at the hem edge or else you will have uneven loops of weft protruding. Dealing with the problem every row by manually knitting the edge stitch is very time-consuming, especially when total knitweave skirts are not exactly produced in a flash anyway.

If you crochet and enjoy doing work as fine as this, then by all means do one row of double crochet (single, USA) and one row of crab stitch (backwards crochet). However, one good way of ensuring that the end stitch only knits and therefore rolls over, is as follows: Knitmaster, use the motif cams, excluding the end stitch and including all else; Brother and Toyota, have the weft yarn beside you, and lay over, excluding the end hem-side stitch on every row.

The tension swatch

For a skirt, I recommend that you knit both a trial swatch and a section. You will require the stitches per 10cm (4in) to calculate the length, and the width in rows of the straight row wedge. I have observed that a common stitch tension in a 2/24s bright acrylic base and a 4-ply synthetic weft is 22.5-23sts per 10cm. T2 approx. I have no real quarrel with the general assumption that 160sts will achieve the average length of 69cm, since 69 x 2.3 = 159sts. I wish to point out, however, that the row count is never the same, especially if you use a wool mix as weft. The range can be as great as 42-58 rows per 10cm. By ignoring the discrepancies involved, you could end up with a skirt shape that is radically different from the one you had intended. You should not forget the significance of the stitch and row ratio in the production of knitted fabric. It is a fundamental principle observed in the industry.

You will need a tension swatch for the top anyway. If you do not have one, and assume that there are common shaping breakdowns for the neck edge and shoulders, then do not be surprised if your garment does not fit; but it need not be rejected, because you can always repair the damage with cut and sew.

Tip for marking the rows in a swatch: there is no need to knit in a contrast yarn; do not weave the two rows before and after 60 rows.

Pressing the trial swatches

You will require a steam iron which emits plenty of steam. Press the work in the row direction of the stitches, which is lengthways across the fabric, and widthways when made up as a skirt. In synthetic fabrics this will be a de-bulking as well as a pressing process. If you overdo it the result is 'overkill'. Press lightly, firmly and evenly, and avoid giving one area more pressure than another or you may produce a blister of melted synthetic, and the garment will be a total disaster. On the hem edge, steam first on the knit side, pat and curl back the edge with your fingers. Steam again to set, and then lightly press.

Leave the fabric to dry and cool before checking the measurement. Providing the knitting and pressing processes have been done correctly, the skirt will not drop in the wearing, because the weft bars hold out the stitches, ensuring that you achieve a low stitch count. On stocking stitch skirts with woven wedges, press across the stitches as well as vertically down the rows to ensure that you get the optimum low stitch count. The wedges will form attractive scallops on the hem edge, evidence that there are fewer stitches per 10cm (4in) and therefore more length than in the stocking stitch flares.

Co-ordinating stripe patterns

On the first outfit I knitted for myself, which incorporated knitweave stripes with stocking stitch, I separated the knitweave stripes on the top by the same number of stocking stitch rows that I had at the waistline of the skirt, i.e. six. The outfit looked as if it were composed of two pieces, top and a skirt in two different patterns, yet the total effect was quite attractive. Now I usually separate the stripes in the top by as many rows as I have at the widest part at the hipline, so that the top and skirt can be one, stripe-wise. On a dress I would follow the same principle, and ease the wider spaces between the stripes on the top into the narrow spaces at the waistline on the skirt. This is for matching and to slenderise the waist, if required. You should knit two swatches, one for the top and one for the skirt, and will need to work out the placement of the stripes on the top at the onset.

Waistbands

An easy waistband

The easiest one of all is to turn over the waist edge and catch down the extra stitches allowed, to form a hem. This method is fine for a simple A-line or fairly straight skirt which is well covered by the top at the waistline, but not ideal for a skirt where we want to emphasise the unpressed pleats, or indeed, where we simply want to be professional in our finish. You may prefer to knitweave a band and apply it separately. You can also have a single-thickness band sewn to waist elastic, and insert a zip if you choose. Here, however, is a good stocking stitch waistband which is quick, easy and looks professional as well. It comes from Betty Abbott's *Machine Knitted Skirts*.

Waistband (two sections)

Pick up the edge stitches, right or wrong side facing, in the pleat formation you require, and using a 3- to 4-ply equivalent MY on stocking stitch (i.e. two ends of fine backing yarn), set the carriage to slip-part-empty. Push out every other needle to HP. Set the cams to knit back. MT+3, knit the row. A slip loop is laid below every other needle. Change to hem tension. Knit depth of hem required. On the last row, pick up the slip loops on every other needle. Knit 1 row optimum tension. Link-latch off.

9 Garment design and the Magic Formula

In recent years it has been very interesting to see different approaches to garment design. Here are some I have identified:

1. The shape is first. The yarn and colour come next. The stitch pattern is the least important.

2. The stitch pattern comes first. The colour and yarn come next. The shape is classic and is least important.

3. Colour and yarn are first. The shape comes next. The stitch pattern is the least important.

4. We buy a pattern and use it as a starting point for our own yarn and stitch ideas. The shape is our version of the one given in the pattern.

This last option has been the way in to creative design for many knitters, and again underlines the principle of moving towards independent design activity by using the ideas of others as a springboard.

Fashion, craft and design

A famous columnist has said that 'fashion is not fashion any more' meaning, presumably, that it is no longer possible to command the public's implicit obedience with regard to major trends and innovations in dress. Far from being free from such pressures, hand and machine knitters are being overwhelmed by publications which claim to be trend-setters merely because they are called by the name 'fashion' or 'designer'. Since the directors of 'fashion' or 'designer' creations cannot themselves agree on a common style for us all, it is not surprising that their efforts should meet with a somewhat muted response.

Here are a few thoughts and questions to help us sort out the confusion and the conflicting demands on our time, money and attention.

1. There are usually general trends which are discernible and which most of us interpret in our own individual ways. Moreover, the machine knitting peer group can set its own styles and fashions, which knitters throughout the world can follow. It is very interesting, however, to note that there are differences in emphases not only worldwide but in a country's regions.

2. A good design that suits us is more important than a short-lived sartorial fad, which may or may not enhance our qualities. If it does the latter, then it is a good design for us, whether or not it is 'fashion'.

3. Though the two words are often used interchangeably, design is 'a plan or scheme in the mind', and a pattern is its practical outworking. Techniques are only starting points and means to an end. They are the servants of the original concept, but how do we choose and use them?

The charting device

Known also as the charter or shaping aid, and going under the brand names of Knit Radar (Knitmaster), Knit Contour (Studio, Singer, USA and Canada), Knitleader (Brother), and KnitTracer (Toyota), the charting device has revolutionised our approach and has made it possible for a great many knitters to draw their own garment blocks and to be free of a written pattern. There is plenty of evidence that charting device knitters buy written patterns, even those without a diagram, for inspiration and ideas. Because charting device knitters work by visual image, they are in charge of the garment from the moment of its conception to its completion.

The charting device is particularly useful in conventional, vertical knitting (from bottom edge to neck), when different parts of the garment are knitted in different stitch patterns, and therefore in a variety of tensions. It is also

109 Lois Franklin 'Degas' pure wool, mohair
and viscose with ribbons woven into body fabric
(courtesy Knitting International)

very useful for fitted sleeve patterns, which are not easy to work out in a straightforward mathematical way. All 'tops' shapes are developed from one of the following three basic blocks: dropped shoulder line, fitted sleeve, and raglan.

The dolman and batwing, so popular at the moment, can evolve from any one of those three (*Fig. 109*). Sweaters and tops, divided into geometric sections, triangles, diamonds, parallelograms and so on, are very easy to develop, and are interesting to knit as well. Certainly the stitch patterns viewed from different angles can be particularly striking. Knitweave responds very well to this treatment. If you want to experiment with garment design and the charting device, it is very important that you have your own collection of basic blocks from which to develop your 'fashion' or 'good design' shape. The choice is yours. A very full account of various aspects of the charting device is given in my *Resource Book Pattern Supplement*, while the last chapter of *Techniques in Machine Knitting* is also devoted to it.

There are situations, however, where the charting device is more of a hindrance than a help, though I would still knit a sideways knitted, fitted sleeve pattern with the aid of the charting device. In this situation, I make a note of any unshaped area not shown on the block (to the left of the dotted line in Fig. 110). Even on a full size Knitleader, one cannot always get the full length widthways on the sheet (see pattern for the suit in Hobby). Once the block is made, it can be pressed into service very quickly on future occasions to suit different yarn and stitch pattern requirements. Moreover, a simple line can alter a shape quite radically.

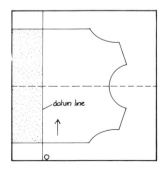

110 Sideways knitted block controlled by the charting device

As we know, flared sideways knitting cannot be planned satisfactorily with the charting device. Sometimes we can work out the breakdown for a sectionalised or sideways knitted dolman more quickly with a calculator and the aid of the Magic Formula, than by drawing on the charter block. The dolman, however, has to be easily broken down into triangles so that the Magic Formula can be used. Triangles and geometric shapes may look angular on a block, but they soften into curves during the knitting process. One can always alter the shaping breakdowns to soften the outline still further, or on a charting device block, turn the underarm straight line curve into the gentle, S-shape dolman sleeve so popular with the Japanese.

The Magic Formula

We could also add 'and the Magic Right-angled Triangle' since the latter is indispensable in the working out of shaping breakdowns on garment blocks as well as on flechages and flares in HP intarsia. However, the triangle is not needed in the working out of stitch reductions in a circular yoke, for instance, nor in the placement of extra sleeve stitches on needles arranged for a cuff. In each case we divide the number of needles we require by the number of extra stitches in order to find out which needles will take the extra ones.

I first read about the Magic Formula, as we call this ingenious way of working out shaping breakdowns, in a Japanese publication, *Knitting Pattern Drafting By Charts* (1976), but it was American machine knitters who were amongst the first to apply the principles of the Magic Formula to working out patterns. Indeed, many pattern writers who have 4-6 sizes to work out would now be lost without the Magic Formula. What we do not know is whether the method originated with the Japanese or Western designers. The Japanese certainly were the first to share a secret which pattern writers have always jealously guarded. After all, when a livelihood is at stake you do not publish the methods by which you earn your living. However, the beans are spilled and the truth is out for the enrichment of us all.

The first important point to stress is that the Magic Formula is employed when we require remainders to be translated into stitches and rows and not decimal fractions. The calculator is used initially to translate centimetres into stitches and rows, with the stitches and rows per 1cm as the two multipliers. At this point, the calculator ceases to be of use, and the Magic Formula takes over. The best way to understand is by a simple example. Note the triangles which represent the increases on both sides of the sleeve outline (*Fig. 111*).

Working out the pattern for a sleeve

Tension: 28sts-40 rows per 10cm (4in).
The multipliers are 2.8 (sts) and 4.0 (rows). In 156 rows we must increase from 62 to 96sts, the difference being 34sts, 17 each side (at the top of each triangle).

Stage 1

$$\frac{9}{17\overline{)156}}$$
$$153$$
$$\overline{3\text{rem}}$$

Stage 2. Put the remainder under the divisor and subtract it.

$$\frac{9}{17\overline{)156}}$$
$$-3153$$
$$\overline{143\text{rem}}$$

Stage 3. Now add 1 to the quotient 9, and you have a remainder of 3, the units of which belong to the next whole number of 10 (9+1). Arrow as shown.

$$\left(\frac{9+1}{17\overline{)156}} \atop {-3153 \atop \overline{143\text{rem}}}\right)$$

The pattern would read: increase 1 stitch at each end of the 9th row 14 times, and at each end of the 10th row 3 times. We check as follows:

$$9\text{x}14 = 126$$
$$10\text{x}3 = 30+$$
$$\overline{156}$$

The Magic Formula is difficult to explain. The best way to understand it is to do several examples mindlessly, following stages 1-3 each

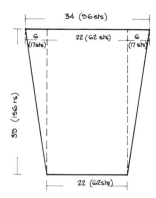

111 The Magic Formula and sleeve triangles

time without trying to fathom out the process. It may help to write out nine, 17 times, and distribute the three remainder as units underneath the first three nines.

Comprehension dawns eventually, but it is much more important to know the procedure off by heart. We eventually acquire tremendous respect for such a simple method that we cannot fault. Acceptance of the Magic Formula, and belief in its reliability, can be compared to the theorem that we learnt at school that the circumference of a circle is $2\pi R$ (R for radius, 2R is the diameter), and that π is used to denote 3.142. It just happened that one of the Ancients found that the formula worked. As you will see from the patterns later on in this chapter, the theorem is as reliable now as it was several thousand years ago.

The Magic Formula and the needle groups in a flechage (Figs. 112 and 113)

The tension of the sample is 23sts and 54 rows per 10cm (4in) at T2.1 on the Knitmaster 700, with Bramwell's Silky as base, and Tweedknit and Ivette as wefts 1 and 2. The yarn brake was at 5 for base and 4 for weft, i.e. tight. The measurement of the sample is 25 x 30 cm, and the pattern is card 1 locked (ORR). First we change the cm into stitches and rows by multiplying 35 by 2.3 and 20 by 5.4 respectively. Use the calculator. Divide the piece lengthways into four equal parts by dotted lines, and draw the diagonal lines of the flechage. Note how they, together with other lines, dotted and unbroken, create right-angled triangles. These are essential for our calculations with the Magic

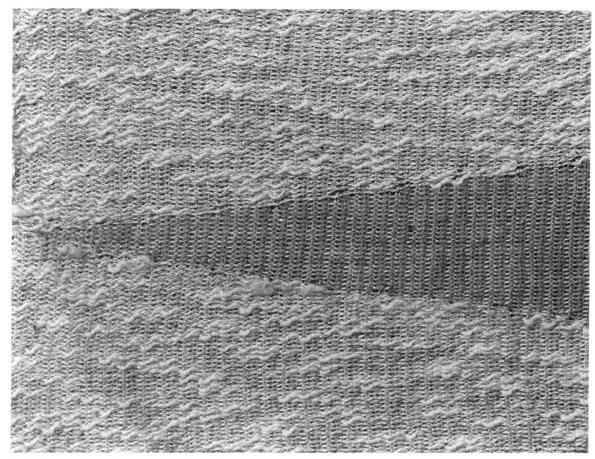

112 Needle groups in a flechage (intarsia knitweave)

Formula. We must have even numbers, since the shaping takes place every alternate row, so sort out the 108 rows into 28, 26, 26, 28. The 28 rows at top and bottom are woven straight. Because we shape every other row, the divisor is 13 and not 26, and the Magic Formula sum is 81 divided by 13. We mark the breakdowns on the bed, beginning from the right, 7 x 3, 6 x 10. You could distribute the 7s among the 6s more equally but the previous arrangement works well on the front of a bodice.

Instructions: T2.1, cast on 81sts. Knit a few rows, carr at right, RC000.
Section A: knit to row 27, carr at left.
Section B: set to hold. Push groups into hold every other row, but one less than marked. On the return journey to the left, put out the final needle to the mark. RC53. Carr at left. Tool back all needles into patterning position. Knit 1 row to the right. RC54.

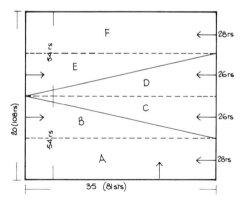

113 Needle groups in the flechage

Section C: RC000. Push out all to hold, except 7+1 needles at right. Change to contrast weft. Knit to left. Push out extra needle to hold. Continue to tool back into patterning position, needle groups plus one needle every alternate row, remembering to push the extra needle to HP for the return row to the right. RC26.

Section D: carr at right. Now at left push out groups to HP, and knit as before. RC54, carr at right. Change back to main weft. RC000. Tool back to patterning position. Knit 1 row to the left.

Section E: push needles out to HP except 6+1 at left. Knit and shape as before. RC26.

Section F: knit final 28 rows without shaping. RC54.

Note: I cast on an extra 5sts at the left, making 86, but these stitches were not counted in the pattern.

Comment

This type of knitting is much easier to do when you knit and follow the markings on the bed for the shaping, but please study the diagram first and try to understand what you are about. The horizontal arrows show the direction of the first row of each section, while the vertical arrow shows the direction of the knitting. We knit the 2 outline rows of the flechage in the main weft because each of the 2 rows smooths out the saw edge and allows the rubbed area from the first lot of HP needles to drop below that of the second. Therefore the same area does not take a beating from the wheels and brushes a second time.

Do try this exercise and you will realise how easy it is to plan and knit arrow-shaped wedges and chevrons on garments.

Note on neck shaping: use a chain method and a piece of spare MY when the carriage is at left. Make a careful note of which shaping needles have disappeared. You still have to knit the rows, but the marks on the bed are there to guide you. In this situation it is easier to do a cut and sew neck.

114 Free-style intarsia and the Knitmaster machine

Free-style intarsia and the Knitmaster machine

Previously I have avoided recommending this technique to Knitmaster knitters because there is no way on their machines in which speedy automatic selection can be used in conjunction with the manual laying on of several yarns across the row.

However, here is a method which I have found quite recently which you can employ on tops and skirts to break the monotony of continuous striping and which is surprisingly quick to do. No pattern card is required. I am delighted that we can now begin to talk about free-style intarsia on garments for all machines. I refer, of course, to knitweave. In this free-style situation we work by laying yarns over the needles and not by the holding position. Indeed there are possibilities for combining various methods.

Instructions: set the Knitmaster machine for the weaving cast on with brushes down, punchcard machines, side levers forward, 560 set to 0. With the 1x1 needle pusher bring eon to HP. Set to knit back. Lay yarns over as required. Knitweave throughout and select with the 1x1 needle pusher every row. On the bottom tab design (*Fig. 114*), I began at the left on the Knitmaster 700, and advanced the contrast weft one needle to the right every alternate row 5 times. I then knitted one more row in the same arrangement before reversing the procedure to the left. RC21. The smaller tab design has 17 rows (8+1+8), and was worked in the same way.

The Magic Formula and the needle groups in a skirt flare

In the UK we tend to think of a number, say 10, 15 or 20, for a needle group which will give us the number of times we want to flare per section, leaving any untouched group at the bottom hemline. It is amazing how successful these 'hit and miss' skirts are, especially if the yarn has a good drape and there is plenty of swing to hide any glaring faults. Certainly, it is a good way for a beginner. Having the same number of needles in the flaring group makes it easy to mark the bed. This method also simplifies the process for a pattern writer. The approach follows in a general way the segment of a circle principle.

A more accurate personalised approach

The Magic Formula can be most useful in working out the needle groups in a flare for the skirt length of your choice as well as for the flare width. As soon as you have worked out the groups to your satisfaction (remembering to check with your hipline requirements), mark the bed with indelible pen. Here is a simple example to follow.

Length 69cm. Waist plus ease 75cm. Number of complete sections with flares 20. Ratio 1:2. Tension 23sts-54 rows at T3, using 2/24s acrylic base and a 2/16s Crossbred wool weft. Pattern 1x1 ORR.

If we flare 6 times in the sequence, that means over 20 rows. As we have explained in Chapter 8, for a complete straightforward flare, the row number must be divisible by 4 not 2, but is 4 less than you expect. For ease, we choose 20 rows. Since our ratio is 1:2, then our straight row wedge is also 20 rows, which measures 3.7cm wide (20 rows at the waist, 40 rows at the bottom edge). If we divide 75cm (waist plus ease) by 3.7cm, the answer is 20.2 complete sections, 20 to the nearest whole number, or 21 if you want it on the full side.

The length is 69cm, which in stitches is 159 (69 x 2.3). We want 6 flares, but we divide by 7 because the last group of all at the bottom hem is not touched by the flare. It remains constant throughout. The Magic Formula sum is 159 divided by 7.

$$22 \quad 22 \quad 23(H) \quad 23 \quad 23 \quad 23 \quad 23$$

H is the hipline. We can easily adjust the flaring groups so that there is a bigger one at the hemline, e.g. 22 x 6, 27. Alternatively, if we wish to drop the flaring to 5 instead of 6, we could run the 6th group with the hem group and leave that constant as well, so the breakdown would be 22 x 5, 49.

All this is, however, hypothetical until you check the hipline, the length and whether the skirt shape is correct for the fabric you have in mind. Once you have done this successfully, there should be nothing to prevent you translating your favourite stocking stitch skirt shape into knitweave. If you can wear fan jumpers (batwings) why not try one of those?

115 Lois Franklin 'Canaletto' (*see* Fig. 3) Note
impact of total look (courtesy Knitting International)

Note on the translation of other stitch patterns to knitweave.

1. Using the stitch and row tension given in the pattern, translate the pattern stitches, rows and shaping sequences back to centimetres.

2. Using the stitches and rows per 1cm produced by your weaving swatch, translate the pattern measurements to the new breakdowns. Use a calculator.

Self-wrap method No. 2

In the first half of the flare, push out to HP one needle fewer than the groups given above. The missing needle will be pushed out to HP on the return row. In the second half, tool back one extra needle, pushing it out to HP again on the return row. If you are knitting stocking stitch flares, you need to use the self-wrap method only once, i.e. when you push out the needles to HP in the first sequence. When you return them, do not include as the last needle on the left of the group, the one that is wrapped. It is, in fact, the first of the next group to be returned. The once-only wrapping closes the hole which would otherwise appear. I have tried this speedier method on total knitweave, but so far have not had complete success. With method 1 recommended in Chapter 8, the marks are uniform and no holes appear, but with method 2 the marks are hardly noticeable. Try both and make your choice.

The Magic Formula, the cape sleeve and polygon shapes (Figs. 116-118)

In the following paragraphs the words segment, flare and flechage are all inter-changeable.

Working towards a circle shape is a most interesting subject large enough to fill another book. Previously I have worked this exercise only in stocking stitch and I am now particularly pleased with the knitweave results. First we take half an octagon as the prototype for a cape sleeve, which could echo the flechage colour changes in the skirt, while the bodice is plain. The long straight side (diameter) represents the measurement all round the armhole (armscye). To illustrate the principle clearly, I have changed colour in the sample every half flare. A full flare is a segment of the circle, divided equally into 8 parts. The full segment is an isosceles triangle. As we

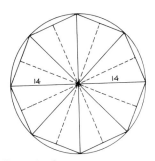

116 The 8 flares in the octagon

know, we can only work out the Magic Formula sum from a right-angled triangle. Two of these make a full segment or isosceles triangle. In the first one, we push needles out to HP, in the second we tool them back to pattern. We need the two processes for the whole flare and this applies whether we have 4, 8, 10, 16 or 20 segments in our circle. Each segment must be halved for calculation breakdowns.

Work out your cape sleeve from the full circle which, incidentally, is a very good shape for a cushion cover. First decide on the depth (diameter) you want. Please note, the breakdowns are different for every diameter. If the cape sleeve is to be inserted into a cut-out on the bodice, add extra to the diameter and curve it round to fit into the armhole. Otherwise you will bite into the curve and take some of its fullness.

Method: Tension 23sts, 54 rows per 10cm, T2.1. Knitmaster 700 with weaving arm. Bramwell's Silky 2/24s and 4-ply acrylic weft. Radius 14cm, diameter 28cm. We need to know the measurement of the circumference and then divide it by 8 for full flare segments.
Circumference = $2 \pi R$ = 2 x 3.142 x 14 = 88cm. Therefore one flare segment is 11cm. We are lucky there are no remainders. However for the breakdowns we need half = 5.5cm. Remember we push out the HP groups and then tool them back, and the two processes together make one flare. It is important to understand this, hence the repetition of the explanation.

Now change the radius into stitches, 14 x 2.3 = 32sts. Change the depth of half a segment to rows, 5.5 x 5.4 = 30 rows to nearest. We must leave at least 2sts untouched by the shaping, so we cast on 32sts and the HP breakdowns are 2sts per every other row 15 times. If the sum had remainders we would allocate them evenly along the row and mark the needle bed where

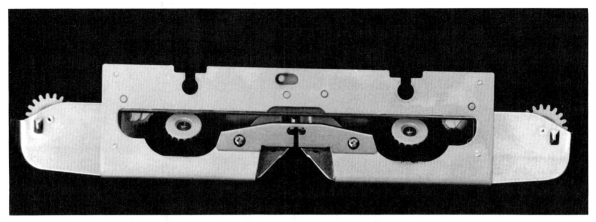

117 The Knitmaster weaving attachment

118 Knitwoven polygon shapes

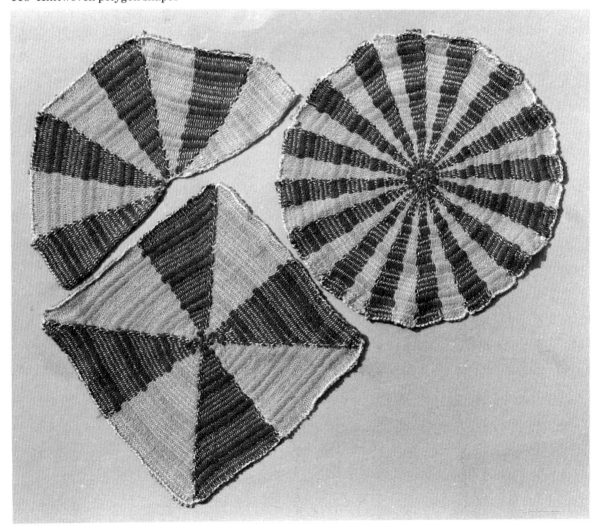

necessary, e.g. 1, 1, 2; 1, 1, 2; 1, 1, 2. I would mark the bed after the 2s. Do try the following exercise. If figures and words mean nothing to you, knit the sample first and then return to the explanation armed with your visual aid.

Instructions: cast on 32sts. Weave 1 row to the right. Set to hold. T2.1. RC000. Push out 1 needle to HP opp. carr. Weave 1 row. Push 1 needle to HP nearest carr. Weave 1 row. (2 needles in 2 rows, self-wrap method). Repeat 2 rows, 15 times in all. RC30. Change weft.

Carr at right. Tool back 3 needles at left. Weave to left. Push 1 needle to HP nearest carr for self-wrap. Weave to right. Repeat 2 rows, 15 times in all. RC60. Repeat full flare, 4 times for cape sleeves, 8 times for octagon cushion. The Knitmaster weaving attachment was a great asset in this exercise (*Fig. 117*).

To knitweave a square
You need double the number of rows for a full flechage, therefore the breakdown is 1 needle every alternate row x 30 = RC60 for half a flare. A full flare = RC120.

To knitweave a 16-sided polygon
You need only half the depth of the octagon segment for a full flare, therefore the breakdown is 4 needles every alternate row. You need 34sts for this one. If you want a near perfect circle, this polygon is a good choice. The smaller the flare, the rounder the shape. This circle shape is sometimes used as a prototype for a sideways knitted yoke.

Diagonal knitweaving and the square (Fig. 119)
As we have observed earlier in the book, a pattern viewed on the diagonal can be very flattering because it appears to give equal value to each part of the figure, softening any problem

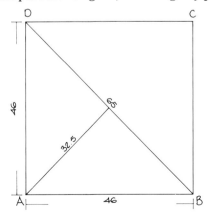

119 Working with the hypotenuse

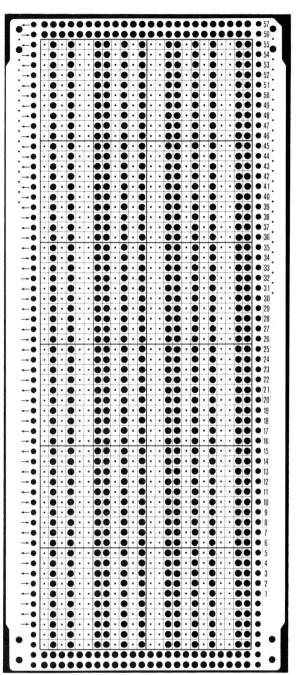

120 Card for Fig. 118

areas and enhancing the most attractive. Some diagonal surface patterns have a dynamism, especially those with protrusions and those which are open-ended. They appear to be unrestricted by boundaries and have no finishing point except at infinity. Others are so bland and regular that they are plainly boring.

I have commented on the difficulties involved in designing diagonal surface patterns. My comments obviously concern one-colour work. If you have a Brother or a Toyota machine, you can introduce diagonal intarsia bands across a horizontally arranged rolling repeat pattern, but that is not my subject here.

Colours and patterns viewed diagonally make a most interesting and refreshing change. If Fair Isle is intriguing done this way, then knitweave is even more so. To view colours and patterns diagonally, we need to use sections based on the right-angled triangle. The square is the easiest garment piece to deal with because the sides are equal and the right-angled triangles are there to help us with the calculations. However, in a square, we need to know the measurement of the diagonal, or the hypotenuse, and so have recourse to another theorem, that of Pythagoras, who deduced that the square on the hypotenuse (DB) of a right-angled triangle (ADB) is equal to the sum of the squares on the other two sides. Then we have to find the square root of that to get the length of the hypotenuse or diagonal DB. If you are confused, draw out your square, full scale, 46x46cm, on newspaper. Cut it out, fold across the middle diagonally and measure the length of the fold. However, with the aid of a calculator, the sum can be worked out from the sketch (*Fig. 120*). To find the hypotenuse (DB), we calculate 46 x 46 = 2116 plus 46 x 46 = 2116 = 4232. The hypotenuse (DB) is the square root of the final figure = 65, half of which is 32.5. In brief, we need the square root of 2 multiplied by the length of one side.

Example: Tension 23sts, 48 rows per 10cm. We turn 32.5 into stitches = 75sts, and 32.5 into rows = 156 rows.

We have to deal with one half (AXB) at a time. The calculations for the other half (AXD) will be the same. Since we must begin with at least 1 stitch for each half (2 for both), we take 1 from 75 = 74. The Magic Formula sum is 156 divided by 74. The instructions would read: cast on 2sts, inc 1 stitch at each end of every 2nd row x 66, and every 3rd row x 8, i.e. along AB and AD. From the centre outwards, DBC, you decrease as you have increased.

I have observed that when the Japanese do this kind of knitting, they often work from the centre (DB) outwards, from the largest to the smallest. Each piece has decreases and not

increases, and there is therefore a much better chance of firm edges and of the two triangles being identical. They are joined on completion along DB.

It is a good idea to distribute the breakdowns evenly. Change colours and border patterns as you proceed and they will appear on the diagonal. Of course it is very simple to draw the square on its apex on the charting device sheet, but the shapings may not be as regular as you would like them. The problem is exactly the same when we come to shape raglan diagonals with the aid of the charting device, and is due entirely to the fact that the charter clicks on every row. The shaping is shown very clearly, but it may not appear in an orderly sequence.

Finally, keep the shaping of such a design to a minimum. You can give any additional length you require to the bottom welt. Alternatively, add a ribbed area for the neck and shoulders or do a cut and sew, or knit in gussets to drop the neckline. The latter method is little used and yet is one of the easiest, most attractive and unobtrusive when incorporated in a pattern as dramatic as this, where you want nothing to detract from its impact.

The skirt hem edge and the Fig. of 8 graft (Figs. 108 and 140)

It is fitting to end with a feature which is indicative of the continuing and exciting work of invention and development. This book is, in more senses than one, just a beginning, a pointer along a way that becomes more fascinating as we travel and progress. Techniques of finishing and making up may seem rather mundane and undeserving of such high-flown language, but if we do not possess the appropriate means of accomplishment we cannot develop the potential of new territory.

A new discovery which came to light just in time to get a mention in the book is the use of the Fig. of 8 graft on a hem edge. Method: with the right side facing and using the three-eyed tool, hook the edge on the needles, 1 stitch deep. Do the graft tightly with the weft yarn or similar. You only need to do a section at a time if you wish. When you return to the machine, support the piece you have edged by hooking up at intervals and continue to pick up the next section to be grafted.

This produces a fine, tight, corded edge, which wraps over the tatty edge weft loops, hiding them completely. Once you can work quickly, you will find this edging is speedier to produce than crochet, and you only go round the bottom circumference of the skirt once.

Teachers in the north-west of England advise that only rarely do students grasp the workings of the Fig. of 8 immediately. Once you are confident, you will work with speed and find the exercise therapeutic as well. We are still completely mystified as to why the Japanese, who are such meticulous finishers, chose to ignore the most beautiful and versatile of edgings and joins. After all, there is no other technique in the whole of our craft culture which can serve as both; neither is there anything which serves the area of knitweave with such consummate perfection.

10 The garment patterns

Abbreviations

alt	alternate
altog	altogether
beg	begin
carr	carriage
CO	cast off
COBH	cast on by hand
cm	centimetre(s)
col	colour
cont	continue
dec	decrease
DK	double knit
eon	every other needle
ev	every
FI	Fair Isle
Fig. of 8	Figure of eight
foll	following
ff	fully fashioned
g	gramme(s)
HP	holding position
in	inch
inc	increase
k	knit
MB	main bed
mm	millimetre(s)
MT	main tension
MT − 1	main tension minus one whole number (example)
MT + 1	main tension plus one whole number (example)
MY	main yarn
n	needle
N1C	needle one cam
NWP	non-working or A position (Japanese machines)
opp	opposite
oz	ounce
patt	pattern
PC	punch or pattern card
RB	ribber
rem	remaining
r	row
RC	row counter

st	stitch (abbreviation never used after 1)
st st	stocking stitch
T	tension (on stitch dial – Japanese machines)
tog	together
UWP	upper working position
WP	working or B position
WY	waste yarn

Preliminary notes

Brand names of knitting machines

Silver Seiko machines are retailed under the following names: Singer – Australia, New Zealand, Canada and parts of northern U.S.A. Studio – USA.
Knitmaster – UK.
Brother machines are retailed under their own label by the Brother distributors in the five English-speaking countries listed above.
Jones + Brother retail Brother machines in the UK, while Knitking also retail them under their own label in the USA. Some Singer-Superba models will do knitweave, and you should check with your manual.

Pattern sizes

The sizes are given in metric. The measurements are all in centimetres. The arrow shows the direction of the knitting, while the zig-zag line indicates where waste yarn is used in sideways, seamless robe knitting.

Sequence shaping

The shaping breakdowns for increases and decreases are calculated by the Magic Formula, and can be checked in the same way. I use the following abbreviated form to convey instructions with economy and speed.
Example: CO the foll sequences at beg of next and ev foll alt row. 7, 3sts x 3, 2, 1 stitch x 3 (21sts dec in 15rs). Knit 11rs etc. You will notice

that I change the RC back to 0 after every section to avoid confusion.

Electronics and the patt repeat

Here is a reminder that you need copy only one repeat of a patt, but for a counterchange or tessellated patt you must also copy the marks for the alternating design in the upper part of PC. You can of course shift the patt by electronic means, but in garment knitting we want to accomplish the piece as speedily as possible. The sts and rs per patt repeat are for your guidance.

Welt instructions

These are given for ribbers only, except for Pattern 2. For a single-bed machine, take 2 or 3 ends of base yarn, or 1 of base, 1 of weft and 1 of nylon thread. Use the 2x1 mock rib setting. Read the instructions for Pattern 2 first.

Memorise-select

These instructions occur at the top of welts and in the sleeve-main piece joins in sideways, seamless robe knitting. The instructions are less applicable to Knitmaster PC machines than to Brother and Toyota, because on the Knitmaster the memory drums pick up the patt every time the carr passes the locked card. On the Brother and Toyota, set the carr to free move slip (part-empty). Take out the base yarn and push the carr to the other end of the bed. Before the return set to patterning slip and the ns will select ready to beg the patt.

Buttonholes in Pattern 2

These are done over groups of 5ns. The best way is the finished method I described in *Techniques in Machine Knitting* (p. 52). The method which is in most manuals concerns the use of 2 lots of WY and the neatening of the buttonholes on completion.

Finally, please re-read Chapters 7, 8 and 9 before you begin. Even if you do not intend to knit any of the garments, I hope sufficient information is given for you to find inspiration and help for your own work in knitweave.

Pattern 1: Child's hooded jacket

Size – 66cm
Measurements – as Fig. 121
Materials – 190g 4-ply Amber Mirage (base). 85g Bramwell's Opal chunky. Thread elastic for welts, 28cm zip

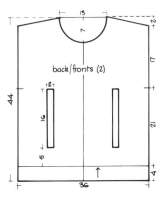

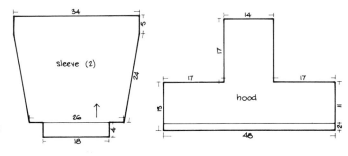

121 Measurements for child's hooded jacket (Pattern 1)

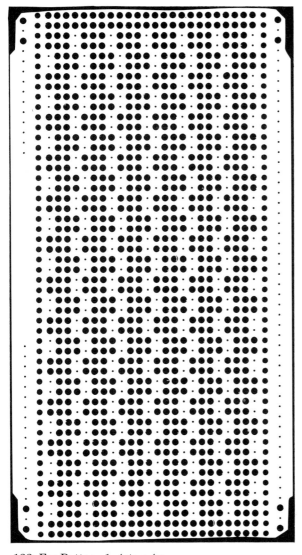

122 For Pattern 1. 4sts x 4rs

Pattern – as Fig. 122. Knitmaster 560. Card 2 (4), Knitmaster Card 4, total knitweave, 4sts x 4rs

Tension square – 24sts x 33rs per 10cm, T4

Machine used – Knitmaster 560 and SRP50 ribber

Notes – Have N1C between 12th and 13th ns on right for left front and between 12th and 13th ns on left for right front

Back

Lock card on r 1 and put on inspection light. Cast on 86sts and arrange for 1x1 rib. T2/3. Taking 1 end of base with 1 end of thread elastic, k 18rs. Remove thread elastic. Transfer RB sts to MB. RC000. T8.1. Prepare to patt. Knitweave 68rs. Mark edges with WY. Knitweave 56rs. RC124. Carr at right.

Shoulder
At beg of next 6rs, CO 3sts. Scrap off on WY 32sts.

Left front

On the right of 0 on the bed, push in WP 44ns. Arrange for 1x1 rib as for back. T2/3. K 18rs. Remove thread elastic. RC000. T8.1. Knitweave 16rs. Carr at right. Note PC row. K 17sts at left with WY (2rs). Then with ravel cord take back to NWP. On 26sts in WP knitweave 52rs. RC68. Now hold 26sts at NWP similarly. Pull back 17sts at left into WP. Turn back card to correct row. Resume pattern knitting. RC 16. Knitweave 52rs. RC68. Break yarn, take carr to right. Mark right edge. RC000. Knitweave to r32.

Front neck

Take 8sts at left onto a piece of WY. Tie and leave. Knitweave 1r to left. CO on next and foll alt rs the sequences 3, 2, 1 stitch x 3. Knitweave to r56.

Shoulder
On next and foll alt rs x 3 CO 9sts.

Right front

As left front, but k 19rs of rib which will bring carr to beg patt at left. Then read left for right and vice versa.

Sleeve (2)

Using WY cast on 62sts. K 6rs. Change to base and weft yarns for knitweave. RC000. Inc 1 stitch at each end of every 8th r x 10. 82sts. RC80. Knitweave to RC96. Scrap off in 8rs of WY.

Hood

Cast on 116sts and arrange for 1x1 rib using base yarn only. K 8rs, T2/3. Arrange for patt. T8.1. RC000. Knitweave 36rs. CO 41sts at right. Knitweave 1r. CO 41sts at left. RC000. Cont on 34sts for 56rs. Scrap off in WY.

123 Pattern 1

Pocket (2)

With k side of front against machine and nearest to side edge, pick up 45sts on slit edge. Using base yarn and T6 k in st st 44rs. T8. K 1r. T6. K 44rs. Turn front and with weave side facing, pick up 45sts on 2nd edge of slit nearest centre. 2sts are on each n. Push ns to HP and set cams to k back. T7. K 1r. Arrange for 1x1 rib. T2/3. K 10rs. T8/9. K 1r. Transfer to MB. Link-latch off.

Cuff (2)

Push 42ns into WP on MB. With right side facing pick up sts below WY at bottom of sleeve, distributing extra sts evenly. T8. Using 1 end of base with thread elastic, k 1r. Transfer alt sts to RB. T2/3. Rib 18rs. T8/9. K 1r. Transfer all sts to MB. Link-latch off. Remove WY.

Front bands (2)

Push 84ns into WP on MB. Cast on with WY. T7. K 6rs. Carr at right. Change to base yarn. T5. K 7rs. T7. 1r. T5. 7rs. Pick up base loops above ravel cord onto ns. T7. K 1r. With k side facing pick up centre front loops evenly. T10. K 1r. Link-latch off. Remove WY.

Making up

Stitch up shoulders and side of hood. Push 106ns into WP on MB. With k side of back facing, hitch on 32sts. Remove WY. Pick up 37sts at each side. With wrong side of hood facing, pick up centre sts first and then those at sides. 2sts hang on each n. Remove WY. Fig. of 8 graft or k 1r on T10 and link-latch off. St sides and tops of pockets. Place sleeves between markers and st all seams. Remove WY. Tack zip into place and st. Steam lightly.

Pattern 2: Teenager's jacket with placket pockets

Size – 76cm
Measurements – as Fig. 124

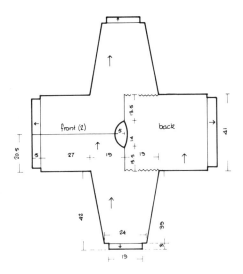

124 Measurements for teenager's jacket with placket pockets (Pattern 2)

Materials – 250g Forsell's 2/16s wool (base), 100g DK wool (weft), 7 buttons, indelible marker
Pattern – as Fig. 125, 12sts, 18rs. Total knitweave, sideways knitted. Seamless robe method, option 3
Tension – 25sts 37rs per 10cm. T7.1
Machine used – Knitmaster 700 with weaving arm
Notes – (1) Single bed welts and st st bands are added on completion of main pieces. The method advocated is ideal for knitweave.

(2) At the top of the first sleeve the maximum number of sts required is 164, i.e. 68 (lower side of front), 48 (half sleeve), 48 (half sleeve). On the bed, push into WP 82ns on each side of 0. Counting from the 82nd n on the left, put a mark between the 68th and 69th ns on the right. Then mark between the 48th and 49th ns to the right of that for the centre of the sleeve. The latter mark should come between the 34th and 35th ns on the right of 0 on the bed.

(3) Back – you require 116sts, i.e. 48 (half sleeve) and 68 (lower side of back). The previous needle-bed arrangement does not work since there are insufficient ns to the right of 0. You

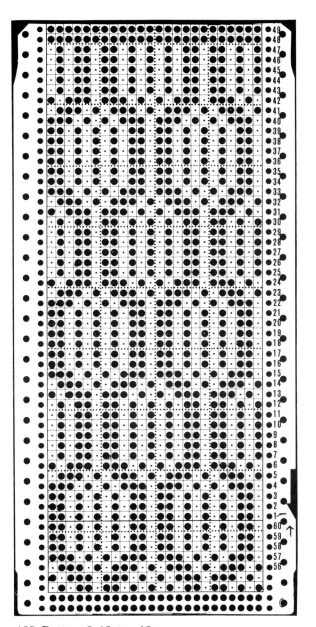

125 Pattern 2. 12sts x 18rs

must begin 3 whole patt widths to the left, away from n33 on the right of 0. Electronic knitters, count the blocks of 24ns carefully. PC knitters can read the repeats easily by the marks on the n strip. You will find that the centre comes between 37 and 38 on the left of 0, and n37 is the first n in the sleeve half for the back. Remove old marks before replacing with new ones.

(4) Always lock or stop the card before you free move or patt slip, and disengage RC.

134

126 Pattern 2

Sleeve – Front – Sleeve

Sleeve 1

Lock card on rl. Counting from the 5th n on the right of 0, push into WP 60ns, 30 on each side of the indelible mark between the 34th and 35th ns. Cast on with WY and k 6rs. Carr at right. Change to base and weft yarns. T7.1. RC000. Prepare to knitweave. Inc 1 stitch at each end of 7th r x 10, 8th r x 8, 96sts. RC134. Weave 10rs straight. Carr at right. Note PC number, and lock card. Check markers on bed. Take 48sts at the extreme left onto WY, and then on the nylon cord back to NWP. Scrap off 48sts at the right with 8rs of WY. Break base and weft. Take carr to left.

Front

Push into WP 68ns to left of 48ns back at NWP. N82 on left of 0 is last WP n. With a piece of spare base yarn COBH (chain) over these 68ns. Tool to B pos. Pull back into WP 48ns at NWP. Remove ravel cord and WY. Set carr to memorise-select. Take to right. RC000. Release card. Insert base and weft. COBH e wrap over 2 extra ns at the right for shoulder seam. RC000. Shape first shoulder. Inc 1 stitch at shoulder edge on 9th r, 8th r x 4 (5sts inc in 41rs). Weave 9rs. RC50. Shape neck. RC000. CO the foll sequences at beg of next and ev alt row. 7, 3sts x 3, 2, 1 stitch x 3 (21sts dec in 15rs). Weave 11rs straight to centre. Carr at right. Lock card and stop PC. Change to WY and st st. Knit 14rs. Resume knitweave in base and weft. Release card. RC26. Weave 12rs. Inc the foll sts at beg of next and ev alt row. 1 stitch x 3, 2, 3sts x 3, RC52. Carr at right. Shape shoulder. RC000. COBH 7 sts at beg of next r, then dec 1 stitch on shoulder edge on 9th r, 8th x 4. Weave 9rs. RC50. Carr at right.

Sleeve 2

Lock card and note number. Break yarn. Take 48sts on left of sleeve back to NWP on ravel cord and WY. Carr set to free move slip, take to left. Scrap off 68sts on right of carr. Release from machine. Push 48ns into WP at right of 48 in NWP. COBH using chain. Tool back to B pos. Pull 48ns to left back into WP (98sts for top of sleeve). Take carr to right on memorise-select. Release card. Resume knitweave. RC000. Insert base and weft. Weave 8rs. Dec 1 stitch at end of next and ev foll 8th r x 8. Weave 7rs. Dec 1 stitch at each end of next and ev foll 8th r x 10. Weave 6rs. Scrap off on WY.

Back

Lock PC on r noted at top of first sleeve. Take carr to right. Beg at the 37th n at left of 0, hitch 48sts at top of first sleeve on to ns. Push up 68ns to right of these 48, and COBH (chain). At left cast on 2sts at shoulder for seam by inc 1ff and leaving an edge n in WP. Set carr to memorise-select and take to left. Release card. RC000. Shape first shoulder as for front, reading left for right. RC50. Carr at left. Shape neck. RC000. CO 5sts at beg of next r and 2sts at beg of foll alt r. Weave to r50 and cast on 2sts at beg of next r. Weave 1r. RC000. COBH 5sts at beg of next r. Shape 2nd shoulder as for front. Check PC. CO extra 2sts at left. Scrap off in 2 sections, 48 and 68sts.

Cuffs

Push 48ns to WP. Cast on with WY. K 7rs. Carr at left. Change to MY. T5. K 1r. Arrange for 2x1 single-bed welt. K 20rs. T7. K 1r. T5. K 20rs. Close welt. Push in-between ns into WP. T7. K 1 r. With wrong side of sleeve facing, hitch 60sts on to 48ns, distributing extra sts evenly. T10. Knit 1r. Link-latch off. Remove WY.

Back welt

As cuff but over 76sts.

Front welts

As cuff but over 38sts.

Neck band

St top shoulder seams. Cut up the centre of the WY. K neckband as for cuffs, but over 110ns.

Button band

As for cuffs but over 132sts and 12rs depth. RC25.

Buttonhole band

As button band but do 7 buttonholes on rs 6 and 19. Each buttonhole is over 5sts. Leave 4sts at bottom and top. Spaces between buttonholes, 15 x 5, 14sts. Complete buttonholes. Remove WY.

Placket pockets (2)

Pick up 40sts just above welt on front, right side facing. T5. RC000. K 40rs. Set to hold. Push to HP 1n nearest carr on next 20rs. Push to UWP 1n nearest carr on next 20rs. K 40rs. RC120. With wrong side of back facing, pick up 40sts onto placket pocket sts. Slip one over the other. Do Fig. of 8, or 1r on T10 and link-latch off. Stitch up sides of pocket.

Making up

Seal back shoulder seam and side seams, using Fig. of 8 or bind off technique. Join underarm seams. St on buttons. Remove WY. Give a light steam and press.

Pattern 3: Lightweight dolman and intarsia panel

Size – 86-91cm
Measurements – as Fig. 127

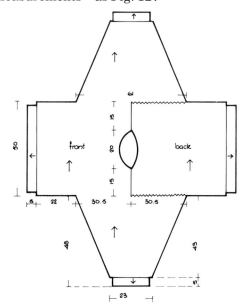

127 Measurements for lightweight dolman with intarsia panel (Pattern 3)

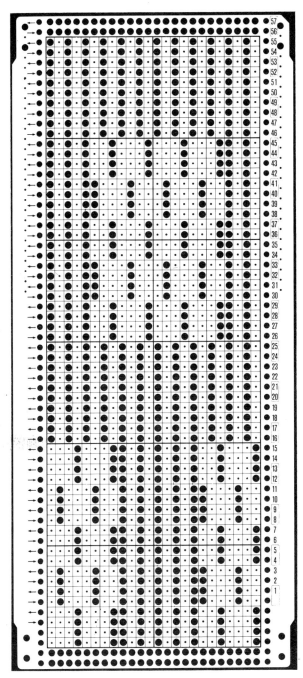

128 Card for Pattern 3. 24sts x 60rs

Materials – 75g Bramwell's Silky (2/24s Bright acrylic) (base), 100g Forsell's 2/16s wool (weft), 25g Amber Fair Isle (multi-coloured 4-ply acrylic) (weft), indelible marker

Pattern – as Fig. 128. 24sts x 60rs. Card locked on r60 for main pattern, and released for intarsia. Total knitweave, sideways knitted, seamless robe method. Option 3

Tension – 23sts, 54rs per 10cm. T3.1

Machine used – Brother 881 plus 850 ribber

Notes – (1) For Knitmaster knitters and/or a speedier alternative to the intarsia patt, change the base yarn underneath the patt blocks to a darker col and smock the weave by lifting the 3st span floats every 4rs on to the centre n.

(2) Please note that the main and intarsia weft yarns are not overlapped because the edge this method creates is untidy. Instead, on completion, turn over the front to the wrong side, and with the work tool crochet up the ladders between the main and intarsia weft. This method closes the gap very neatly and is quick to do.

(3) There are two patts, the card 1 ORR weave (last 10 rows of card), and the panel patt. Electronic knitters, treat them as 2 separate patts and move from one to the other as required. PC owners can also punch the card as Fig. 7, but see that the selection matches. It is very easy to match the card 1 ORR patt because there are only two sts. Nevertheless, check that the sts for the back co-ordinate with those to which they are to be joined on the front.

(4) For the intarsia patt I used 10 spring-clip clothes pegs, 5 for each weft, and wound a small amount of yarn on each. I laid the yarn over the appropriate ns as selected and left sufficient yarn unwound to be woven in. It is important to keep the edges as neat as possible by hooking the most appropriate weft into the nearest ns to close the gap every other row.

Sleeve – Front – Sleeve

Lock the card on r60. With the extra n on the right, first mark the bed over 191ns, 51, 70, 70. The sleeve centre comes between ns 26 and 27 on the right of 0. Counting from n4 left and n56 right, push into WP 60ns. Using WY, k 6rs. Carr at right. Change to base and main weft for knitweave. RC000. T3.1. Inc 1 stitch at each end of 5th r x 8, 6th r x 32. RC232. 140sts. Weave 2rs. Carr at right. Break yarn. Card stays locked. Take 70sts at left back to NWP and on nylon cord. Scrap off 70sts on right on WY. Take carr to left. With a piece of base yarn COBH (chain) over 51ns at left of those in NWP. Tool back to B pos. Pull 70ns back into WP. Carr set to

129 Pattern 3

memorise-select. Take to right. Insert base yarn. Inc 2sts at right for shoulder seam. RC000. Continue knitweaving to RC84. RC000. At beg of next and alt r CO 6, 2sts. Knitweave to RC93. Release card and lock on rl. Next r, memorise-select. Release card. Start intarsia pattern after r94. On r100, cast on 2sts, on r102, cast on 6sts. RC000. Knitweave to RC84. At the same time on completion of 3 blocks of patt, return to card 1 ORR pattern. Card stays locked. CO 2 extra sts at right edge. Break yarn. Take back 70sts on left sleeve half to NWP on WY and ravel cord. Scrap off 51sts on left on WY. Carr at left. With a piece of spare main yarn base COBH (chain) over 70ns to right of those at NWP. Tool back to B pos. Pull 70ns held at NWP back into WP. Carr set to memorise-select. Take to right. Insert base yarn. RC000. Continue knitweaving in main weft. Weave 2rs. Dec 1 stitch at each end of next r and every 6th r x 32, weave 5rs. Dec 1 stitch at each end of next r and every foll 5th r x 8. Weave 4rs. RC234. 60sts remain. * Using weft, base and nylon thread, k 1r at T4.1. Transfer alt sts to RB. T0/1. Rib 31rs. Carr at right. T9/8. K 1r. Transfer all sts to MB. Link-latch off. For 2nd cuff, with right side facing, pick up sts from first sleeve and repeat from *. Remove WY.

Back

Carr on left. Begin at n61 on left. Push into WP 121ns, extra n on left. Mark the bed 70-51. Starting at left and right side facing, hitch on 70sts from right half of first sleeve. Remove WY. COBH (chain) over 51ns at right. Tool back to B pos. Inc 2sts at left for seam. Set carr to memorise-select. Take to right. T3.1. Insert base yarn. RC000. Knitweave 84rs. RC000. CO 4sts. Weave 104rs. COBH 4sts. Weave 84rs. CO 2sts at left. Scrap off in WY in 2 sections, 70 sts and 51sts.

Welts for back and front

Pick up 118sts and foll instructions for cuffs.

Making up

Seal vertical back shoulder seam, welts and side seams, using Fig. of 8 graft or bind off technique. Stitch underarm seams. Neaten intarsia. Remove all WY.

Double roll neck edgings

Back: first roll. Wrong side facing, carr at right.

Pick up 70sts. Push up 1 extra n at each side. 72sts. Using 1 end of weft and 1 end of base, T5, k 1r, T4, 3rs, T7, 1r. Link off. Second roll. Wrong side facing, pick up base of sts of first roll. T4. K 5rs. Link off. Front as back but over 82 + 2sts. Stitch at edges and give a light steam press.

Pattern 4: Paisley patterned dolman

Size – 86-91cm
Measurements – as Fig. 127 in previous patt

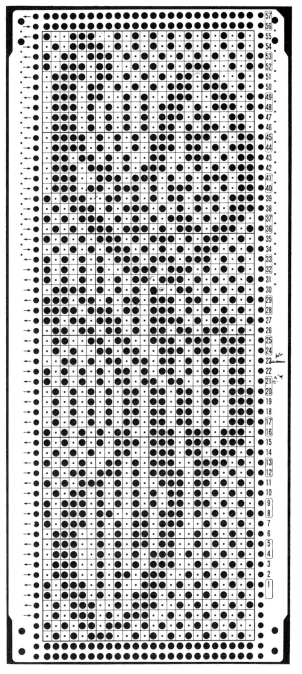

130 Card for Pattern 4. 24sts x 60rs

Materials – 150g of 2x2/30 acrylic (2-ply) (base), 150g of 4-ply acrylic (weft), indelible marker
Pattern – as Fig. 130, 24sts x 60rs, total knitweave, sideways knitted as previous patt
Tension – 23.5sts, 47r per 10cm (4in). T5
Machine used – Knitmaster 700 with weaving arm and SRP50 ribber
Notes – (1) Because nearly the whole length of the bed is in use at the top of the sleeve (195sts), I could not use the weaving arm. When I changed back to the normal assembly unit, I tightened the yarn brake one point to keep the tension balanced.

(2) Though the r tensions differ considerably in knitweave, the st tension of around 23sts occurs again and again, even though different yarns are used over a wide range of dial numbers. One is forced to the conclusion that the n spacing of 4.5mm has something to do with it. It would be interesting to know how the Singer Superba (5mm) performs in these circumstances.

Sleeve – Front – Sleeve

Lock the card on r1. First mark the bed over 195n, 51, 72, 72, having 95 at left and 100 right of 0. The sleeve centre comes between ns 28 and 29 on right of 0. Counting from n2 on left and moving towards 60 on right, push into WP 62ns. Using WY k 6rs. Change to base and weft. RC000. T5. Release card for knitweave. Inc 1 stitch at each end of 5th r x 36, 4th r x 5. RC200. Knitweave 2rs. 144sts. Note PC and position in patt repeat at first n at right of centre, i.e. 29.

  Carr at right. Break yarns. Lock card. Take 72sts at left back to NWP on WY and nylon cord. Scrap off 72sts at right on WY. Take carr to left. With a spare piece of base yarn COBH (chain) over 51ns at left. Tool back to B pos. Pull 72ns back into WP. Carr set to memorise-select. Take to right. Insert base and weft yarns. Inc 2sts at right for shoulder seam. RC000. Continue knitweaving to RC72. RC000. At beg of next and alt rs CO 8,4,2sts. Weave to RC90. At beg of next and alt rs, COBH (e wrap) 2,4sts. Knitweave to RC94. RC000. COBH 8sts. Knitweave to RC72. Lock card and note PC row. CO 2 extra sts at right edge. Break yarn. Take 72sts on left sleeve back to NWP on WY and nylon cord. Scrap off 51sts at left on WY. Carr at left. With a piece of spare MY base COBH (chain) on 72ns on right of those at NWP. Tool back to B pos. Pull 72ns held at NWP back into WP. Carr set to memorise-

select. Take to right. Insert base and weft yarns. RC000. Release card. Cont knitweaving for 2rs. Dec 1 stitch at each end of next r and ev foll 4th r x 5. Knit 3rs. Dec 1 stitch at each end of next and ev foll 5th r x 36. Knit 4rs. RC202. 62sts. Transfer for 1x1 rib. Using 2 ends of weft and nylon thread, T1/2, k 24rs. T10/10. K 1r. Transfer to MB. Link-latch off.

Other cuff
With wrong side facing, pick up 62sts on MB. Transfer for 1x1 rib. K as above. Remove WY.

Back

Carr at left. Beg at n68 left of 0. Push into WP 123ns. Mark the bed 72,51. Last one on right is 55. Starting at left with right side facing, hitch on 72sts from right half of first sleeve. Remove WY. COBH (chain) over 51ns at right. Tool back to B. Inc 2sts at left for seam. Set carr to memorise-select. Take to right. T5. Insert base and weft. RC000. Knitweave 72rs. RC000. CO at beg of next and foll alt rs 4,1,1sts. Weave to RC90. At beg of next and foll alt r COBH 1,4sts. Knit 1r. RC000. COBH 4sts. Knitweave 72rs. CO 2sts at left. Scrap off in WY 2 sections 72 and 51sts.

Welts for back and front

Carr at left. With wrong side facing, pick up 135 edge loops. T7. K to right with 2 ends of weft and nylon thread. Transfer for 1x1 rib. RC000. T2/3. K 6rs. T1/2. K 34rs. RC40. T10/10. K 1r. Transfer to MB. Link-latch off.

Picot neck trim

St up shoulder seams.

Back
Carr at right. With wrong side facing pick up 60 edge loops. Knit ev alt st by hand loosely. T5. 2 ends of weft, k 4rs. Change to base. K 1r. Transfer ev alt st to its neighbour leaving empty ns in WP. K 1r. Change to weft. K 5rs. Pick up loops below and place on alt ns. T10. K 1r. Link-latch off.

Front
As back, but over 90sts.

Making up

Seal vertical back shoulder seam, welts and side seams, using Fig. of 8 graft or bind off technique. St underarm seams. Remove all WY. Give a light steam. No pressing.

Pattern 5: Mohair sweater in lacy knitweave

Size – 86-91cm
Measurements – as Fig. 132

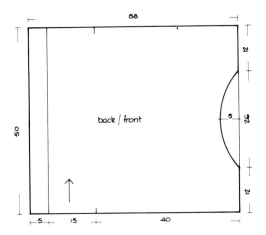

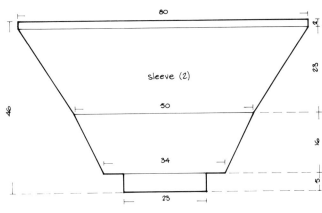

132 Measurements for mohair sweater in lacy knitweave (Pattern 5)

Materials – 125g Hobby 2-ply acrylic nylon knop (base), 150g variegated mohair (top quality handknit) (weft), 50g matching 4-ply wool, crochet hook
Pattern – Card 1 (rolling repeat). Electronics – pattern 1, sheet 1. 2sts. 2rs.
Needle arrangement – 2 WP, 2 NWP. Total knitweave. Separate sleeves. Back, front, sideways knitted. Option 2
Tension – 24sts, 34.5rs per 10cm. T8
Machine used – Brother 910 and 850 ribber
Notes – (1) Put the mohair in the refrigerator the night before you intend to knit, or in the freezer for half an hour. Hang tension swatches on the sinker pins. Pull swatches down out of harm's way. These are precautions against the mohair sticking on the metal. Having to wrench the mohair away from the pins every few rows thoroughly destroys one's enjoyment of knitting this most beautiful of fabrics.

(2) In Chapter 7, option 2, I omitted to point out that with a simple 1x1 pattern, all one needs to do when knitting the second sleeve is to move the arrangement 1 stitch to the left or right, since we are dealing with a 2st, 2r patt. The top of the sleeve will then match perfectly at the join. In any case, this variegated mohair is so fluffy that it hides any mistakes in the join.

(3) The ns at NWP are counted as sts throughout. When inc or dec, break the n arrangement by drawing into the complement ns at the edge which should be in NWP. Move out the ns and create the n arrangement as you shape. The neck shaping is done at the right on the front, and on the left on the back to ensure pattern matching at the shoulders and to co-ordinate with the sleeve tops.

Sleeve 1

Lock card on r1. Push into WP 79ns. 39 on either side of 0. Take back into NWP the 3rd and 4th and ev foll 3rd and 4th n. Cast on with WY. K 8rs. Carr at right. RC000. T8. Change to base and weft. Prepare to knitweave. Inc 1 stitch at end of 3rd r x 30, and at each end of 2nd r x 23. RC36. 184sts. K 6rs. Note whether n1 left and right of 0 has selected or not. the card should show an odd number for the next r to be knitted. Scrap off in 8rs of WY.

Sleeve 2

As sleeve 1 but arrange 78ns as 40 and 38 on left and right of 0.

Sleeve cuff (2)

Carr at left. With wrong side facing, pick up 61sts (2 st loops and 1 bar). Inc 1 stitch at each side. 63sts. Using 4-ply matching wool, T7, k 1r. Transfer for 1x1 rib. T2/3. 10rs. T1/2 19rs. T10/8 1r. Transfer to MB. Link off.

Front

Push into WP 123ns, 62 at the left and 61 at right of 0. Check with sleeve top for co-ordination. Knit 7rs WY. Carr at left. Break WY. Using base, COBH (chain) over 31ns at

133 Pattern 5

extreme left. Break yarn. COBH (chain) over rem 92ns. Tool back to B pos. Lock card on odd number. Memorise-select and take carr to right. Change to base and weft. Prepare to knitweave. Release card. At right COBH (e wrap) over 2 extra ns for the shoulder seam. RC000. Knitweave straight to RC42. RC000. * At beg of next and foll alt rs, CO 4,3,2,1 stitch x 3. Cont to RC80. At beg of next and foll alt rs, inc 1 stitch x 3,2,3. K 1r. RC90. RC000. Inc 4sts at beg of next r. ** K to RC42. CO 2 extra sts at the right. Scrap off on 8rs of WY, 2 lots over 31 and 92 sts.

Back

Foll instructions for front to *, but beg with 8rs of WY and read right for left and vice versa.

Neck shaping
At beg of next and foll alt rs, CO 2, 1 stitch x 2. K to RC86. At beg of next and foll alt rs, inc 1 stitch x 2. K 1r. RC000. COBH (e wrap) 2sts. Cont from ** to end.

Back-front welts

Carr at left. With wrong side of bottom edge facing, pick up 131 edge loops. Using 4-ply wool, T7, k 1r. Transfer for 1x1 rib. T1/2, 34rs. T1/1, 5rs. T10/8, k 1r. Transfer to MB. Link-latch off.

Making up

St shoulder seams. Do 2rs double crochet (single, USA), on neck edge with 4-ply wool. Join sleeves to back-front. Make extra chains for spaces. Draw tog with strands of Hobby. Alternatively, use the work tool and crochet CO method, chaining extra loops across the gaps. Seal side seams in same way. Remove WY. St underarm and welt seams. Do not press.

Pattern 6: Kaleidoscope multicoloured sweater

Size – 86-91cm
Measurements – as Fig. 134
Materials – Back, sleeve and welts – 200g Bramwell's Astrakan and 2-ply Botany taken tog for a 4-ply equivalent. Front – 75g of 4 base yarns (2-ply). 100g of 9 weft yarns (4-ply). Nylon thread
Patterns – Back and sleeve – st st. Front – knitweave patterns, illustrated in Fig. 135. 24sts, 63rs

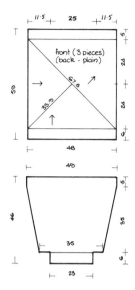

134 Measurements for the kaleidoscope multicoloured sweater (Pattern 6)

Tensions – St st 26sts, 38rs per 10cm. T8
Knitweave – 25sts, 55rs per 10cm. T2.1
Machine used – Brother 881 and 850 ribber
Notes – (1) Change the 4 base and weft yarns in order. Because there are 9 weft yarns, there is a different permutation the next time round. Hence the name Kaleidoscope. If you do not want to deal with so many yarns, try black, white and 2 shades of grey (*Fig. 136*) for a different but very striking effect, or indeed any mix of your choosing. The pattern is an excellent way of using up yarn oddments, but please sample them on your tension swatch first.

(2) Though I give the decreasing breakdowns for those who prefer to shape, the triangles on the front were done by cut and sew for speed and efficiency. Cast on the number of sts and k the depth in rs required for each triangle. Cut out cardboard shapes to match, allowing 5mm extra for seams. The seams can be easily stitched by a sewing machine with a simple zig-zag facility (do twice), though I used the Frister Knitlock 5 on the garment here.

Front

Large triangle
Lock card on r1. Push 170ns (174 cut and sew) into WP. Cast on with WY. Carr at right. Change to first base yarn. COBH (e wrap) over WY. MT+1. K 1r. T2.1. Memorise-select. K 1r to

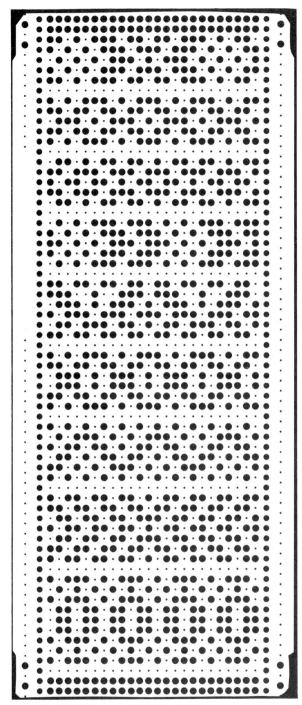

135 Card for Pattern 6. 24sts x 63rs

Small triangle (2)

Lock card. Push 120ns into WP (124 for cut and sew). Cast on with WY. Knit 8rs. Carr at right. Change to first base yarn. COBH (e wrap) over WY. MT+1. K 1r. T2.1. Memorise-select. K to right. RC000. Release card and beg st st and knitweave patterns as for large triangle. At the same time dec 1 stitch at each end of 2nd r x 3. Dec 1 stitch at each end of 3rd r once. Repeat 9r sequence x 14. RC126. Dec 1 stitch at each end of 2nd r x 3. RC132. CO 2sts. For cut and sew k straight to RC134.

Back

Push 124ns into WP. Arrange for 1x1 rib, using Botany and Astrakan tog. K 26rs on T1/2. Transfer to MB. Set for st st. T8. RC000. K 110rs. Mark at each end for sleeves. RC000. K 68rs. Transfer for 1x1 rib. T1/2. Rib 20rs. T10/8. K 1r. Transfer to MB. Link-latch off.

Sleeve (2)

Push 90ns into WP. Cast on with WY. K 6rs. Change to MY for st st. T8. RC000. Inc 1 stitch at each end of 7th r x 10, 8th r x 8. RC134. 126sts. K 16rs straight. K 1r on T10. Link-latch off.

Cuffs (2)

Push 60ns into WP. Pick up sts from base of sleeve, putting 2sts on ev 3rd n. T1/2. K 26rs 1x1 rib. T10/8. K 1r. Transfer to MB. Link-latch off. Remove WY.

Bottom front welt

St triangles as shown. K welt as for back. Transfer to MB. With wrong side facing, pick up loops from bottom triangle onto needles, 2sts per n. Fig. of 8 graft off. Remove WY.

Top front welt

Carr at left. Push 124ns into WP. Wrong side facing, pick up loops from top triangle. MT+1. K 1r. Complete welt as for back.

Cut and sew – poke ns through fabric below sewn edge. K the r by hand loosely. Complete welt as for back.

Making up

St shoulders, leaving 25cm open at centre for neck. Insert sleeve. St sides and welt, removing any waste yarn. Steam and press lightly.

right. RC000. Release card and beg st st and knitweave patts. At the same time, dec 1 stitch at each end of the 2nd r x 3. Dec 1 stitch at each end of the 3rd r once. Repeat 9r sequence x 20. RC180. Dec 1 stitch at each end of the 2nd r x 4. RC188. CO 2sts. For cut and sew, k straight to r190. Scrap off.

136 Border patterns in black, grey and white

Pattern 7: Batwing dress with cummerbund waist

Size – 86-91cm
Measurements – as Fig. 137
Materials – 250g 2/24s Bramwell's Silky (base),
350g Patsy Amanda crêpe (3-ply weft)
Patterns – Card 1 ORR and chevron as Fig. 139.
12sts, 21rs. Total knitweave. Top according to
option 1
Tension – Card 1 ORR pressed out for skirt.
22.5sts, 55rs per 10cm. T2. For top, 23sts and
66rs. Chevron rolling repeat. 23sts, 57rs
Machine used – Brother 910 and 850 ribber
Notes – (1) Have yarn brake at tightest and use
yarn support wire and wax. Check that the tuck
wheels are out of action and use a self-wrap
method for shaping the flares in the skirt.

(2) Mark the bed in blocks of 22 x 6, to avoid
confusion.

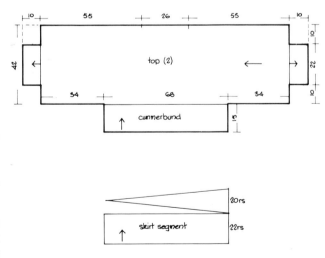

137 Measurements for batwing dress with
cummerbund waist

138 Pattern 6

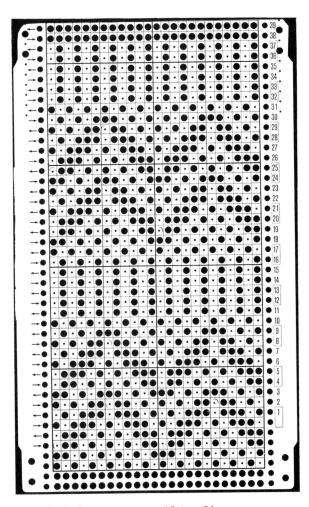

139 Card chevron pattern. 12sts x 21rs

22ns in HP. Weave to right. Repeat x 6 altog. 132ns are in HP. Second half. Tool back 23ns nearest carr into WP. Brother-Toyota – select 1x1 manually. Weave to left. Push WPn nearest carr back into HP. 22ns in WP. Repeat until all ns are in WP. Weave 20rs straight. **. Repeat from * to **, x 24. Work 1 more flare. K 10rs straight. Scrap off in WY.

Making up

With right side facing, hitch up cast on chains on to ns. With wrong side facing, place sts from last row on top. Slip chains over sts. Fig. of 8 graft. Remove WY. Fig. of 8 trim for bottom edge.

Wrong side facing, pick up a whole st and place on ns. Pick up about 50 at a time. Do Fig. of 8 all round bottom using weft yarn. Hot damp press firmly. Fold in half and mark sides at waist.

Top (2)

Lock the chevron patt in machine. With WY, cast on over 96sts. K 6rs. Change to base and weft for patt. Release card. RC000. Knitweave to RC335. Carr at left. Change to card 1 ORR. RC000. Weave to RC106. Change back to chevron patt. RC000. Weave to RC335. Scrap off in WY. Press lightly. Mark at sides for edges of cummerbund.

Cuffs (2)

St shoulder seams, leaving open 26cm on each piece for neck. Turn in 1cm on neck edge and catch down. Carr at left. Push 64ns into WP. With right side of top facing, pick up sts on sleeve, distributing extra sts evenly. T5. K 1r, using weft and 1 end of nylon thread. Arrange for 1x1 rib. T1/1. K 50rs. T10/8. K 1r. Transfer to MB. Link-latch off.

Cummerbund (2)

Push 126ns into WP. Arrange for 1x1 rib. Using weft yarn and 1 end of nylon thread, T1/1, k 70rs. With wrong side of back facing, pick up edge loops on bottom evenly, working from centre outwards towards markers. Fig. of 8 graft off. Do same for front. To attach to skirt, pick up bottom loops of back of cummerbund onto 126ns. Hitch edge loops of skirt evenly, working from centre outwards towards markers. Fig. of 8 graft off. Do same for front. Remove all WY. St underarm seams. Give final press.

(3) The chevron design incorporates sections of the card 1 ORR patt so that the patts in the top and skirt are co-ordinated. Note how the chevron patt is designed to get rid of long floats. Even so the fabric is very silky, and the floats on the sleeve can pull. If they do they can be drawn back easily and invisibly.

Skirt

Lock card 1 ORR patt in machine. Push 154ns into WP. Check that the n at the hem edge selects. Cast on with WY. K 7rs. Carr at left. With piece of base yarn, COBH (chain). Set cam to memorise-select on slip-part-empty. Take to right. RC000. T2. Insert base yarn and prepare to knitweave. At RC12, set to hold. Flare – self-wrap method. First half. * Push out 21ns to HP. Weave to left. Push out 1 more n at carr side.

140 Pattern 7

Pattern 8: Top and pleated skirt in striped knitweave

Size – 86-91cm
Measurements – as Fig. 141
Materials – 400g Hobby (light green) base, 150g mixed 4-ply weft, 25g crisp yarn for neck edge, elastic for waist, indelible marker
Pattern – sideways knitted, alternating stripes of st st and knitweave, Card 1 ORR as Fig. 7.
Knitweave sequence – (20rs) 4rs Amber Mirage (pearlised green), 2rs Fluffy almond green loop yarn, 2rs apricot Hobby with green lurex thread, 4rs tuck (main), 2rs apricot Hobby with green lurex thread, 2rs Fluffy almond green loop yarn, 4rs Amber Mirage (pearlised green)
Tension – Top – 20rs of patt, 10rs of st st sequence. 25sts, 65rs per 10cm. T2.1. Skirt – 20rs of patt, 4rs of st st at waist. Pleated and stitched down – 3.2cm
Machine used – Toyota 901
Notes – (1) Care must be taken to plan the knitweave stripes centrally before the knitting begins on the top.

(2) There is no need to pleat the skirt if you prefer not to do so. An unpleated skirt with 25 panels will fit a size 106cm hip, and you need to adjust accordingly.

(3) It has not been possible to adhere rigidly to the terms k and weave in shaping sequences for the top. Be guided entirely by the pattern sequences of 20rs knitweave and 10rs st st.

(4) Remember you are knitting a fitted sleeve sideways. It is easier to write out the shaping sequences in full, and easiest of all to draw on your charting device sheet.

(5) The neck edging trim in Patsy Amanda looks good on either side. It is one of the quickest and most effective I have ever done.

Top

Front

Push out 90ns to WP. Cast on with WY. K 8rs. Carr at right. Using MY, COBH (chain) T2.1. RC000. Insert and lock card. K 10rs st st. Carr at right. Cont in patt of 20rs knitweave and 10rs st st throughout. At the same time: at r10 with carr at right, inc 1 stitch at beg of next row. K 3rs x 2. Inc 1 stitch at beg of next and foll alt rs x 2, k 1r. Inc 2sts at beg of next r. K 1r. Inc 3sts at beg of next and foll alt r x 3 (15sts increased in 19rs). K 1r. RC30. COBH 33sts. 138sts altog.

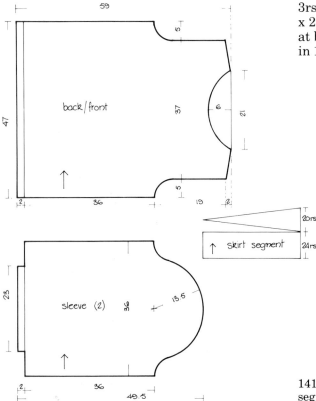

141 Measurements for top with pleated skirt segment in striped knitweave with st st (Pattern 8)

143 Close-up of neck trim

* Shape first shoulder. RC000. Inc 1 stitch at beg of 10th r, and ev foll 12th r x 6. K 2rs. RC84.

Neck
RC000. At the neck edge, cast off the foll sequences on next and ev foll alt r. 6, 3sts x 2, 2, 1. K straight to r126. At beg of neck edge on next and ev foll alt r cast on 1, 2, 3sts x 2. K 1r. Carr at right.

Second shoulder
RC000. At beg of next r cast on 6sts. ** At the same time knit 2rs. Dec 1 stitch at shoulder edge of next r and ev foll 12th r x 7 altog. Knit 10rs. RC000. Cast off 33sts at beg of next r. K 1r. Dec 3sts at beg of next and ev foll alt r x 3. K 1r. Dec 2sts at beg of next r. K 1r. Dec 1 stitch at beg of next and foll alt rs x 2. K 1r. Dec 1 stitch at beg of next r. K 3r x 2. Carr at right. K 10rs. RC32. 90sts. Scrap off in 8rs of WY.

Back
As front to *.

Neck
RC000. At neck edge, on next and foll alt r, CO 3, 2sts. K straight to RC134. At beg of next r, cast on 2sts. K 1r.

Shoulder
RC000. At beg of next r, cast on 3sts. Cont from ** to end.

Sleeve (2)
Push into WP 90ns. Cast on with WY. K 8rs. Lock card. Using MY COBH (chain). Carr at right. RC000. K 10rs. Cont in patt. At the time, on the sleeve cap side only, inc 1 stitch at beg of next 2rs. K 2rs. Inc 1 stitch at beg of next 2rs. K 6rs. Repeat last 8rs twice. Inc 1 stitch at beg of next 2rs. K 4rs. Inc 1 stitch at beg of next 2rs. K 2rs. Repeat last 10rs twice. Inc 1 stitch at beg of next 2rs. K 2rs. Repeat last 4rs twice. Inc 1 stitch at beg of next 4rs. Inc 1 stitch at beg of next 2rs. K 2rs. Repeat twice. Inc 1 stitch at beg of next 2rs. K 4rs. Inc 1 stitch at beg of next 2rs.

K 6rs. Inc 1 stitch at beg of next 2rs. K 10rs. RC98. Inc 1 stitch at beg of next 2rs. K 14rs straight (centre). 124sts. RC134. RC000. Now read the instructions in reverse for the 2nd half of the sleeve cap shaping, reading dec for inc. Scrap off in 8rs of WY.

Hem bottom edge (2)
Carr at right. With wrong side facing, pick up 126sts. Using 1 end of Hobby, T5. K 1r. T9. K 1r slip over eon. T3. K 9rs. T6. K 1r. T3. K 8rs. Pick up slipped loops on to eon. T9. Link-latch off.

Cuffs (2)
With wrong side facing, pick up 60sts, and follow instructions for bottom edges.

Cord
Cast on 4sts. Set for cord knitting. T4. K until long enough to tie round waist.

Neckline edging
St up shoulder seams.
Back – lock card 1 rolling repeat in machine. Carr at right. With crisp yarn, and with right side facing, pick up 84sts, * and chain needles. T5. K 1r to left. RC000. Release card and set to elongation and tuck. T4. K 8rs. Carr at left. Lock card. Change to slip. K 4rs on T5. Set to st st. K to right. RC13. T10. Knit 1r. Link-latch off. Front – as from * but over 106sts.

Making up
Steam press lightly. St shoulders and insert sleeves. St all seams, leaving gap in bottom hem for cord.

Skirt
Lock card in machine. Push 175ns into WP. Cast on with WY. K 7rs. Carr at right. T2.1. COBH (chain). Set carr to memorise-select. K 1r in MY. Carr at left. RC000. Knitweave 20rs of patt. K 1r to the right. Set to hold. Flare 6 times, 25ns per time, as patt 7. K 1r to left. Repeat knitweave patt. Do 25 complete sections of 1r st st, 20rs patt, 3rs st st plus 20rs st st flare. After last flare, scrap off in WY. St down one side of each patt. Make up as Pattern 7.

Waist hem (2)
With wrong side facing, carr at right, pick up 106sts. Using 1 end of Hobby, k 1r of 1x1 slip on T9. T3. K 13rs. T6. K 1r. T3. K 12rs. Carr at right. Pick up loops on eon. T9. K 1r. Link-latch off. Insert elastic. Give final press.

Pattern 9:
Shorty top in smocked knitweave

Size – 86-91cm
Measurements – as Fig. 144

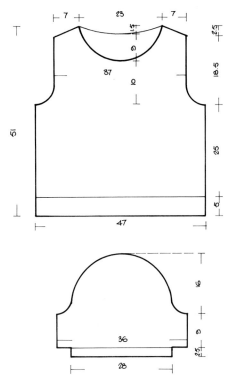

144 Measurements for shorty top in smocked knitweave (Pattern 9)

Materials – 150g Ambergora 3-ply, 50g 4-ply lurex, beads optional
Pattern – as Fig. 145. 8sts x 14rs, 5rs knitweave, 2rs st st in counterchange patt. On r3, smock by lifting up 3 lurex loops on to centre n. Beading optional on top half of sleeve and yoke.
Tension – 27.5sts, 45rs per 10cm on T6
Machine used – Brother 910 and 850 ribber
Notes – (1) You can make this top as long as you please, but consider the proportions provided by the neckline and puffed sleeves. Do add shoulder pads if you wish. You can k your own and stuff with shredded tension swatch.

(2) The beads, unfortunately, do not show up in the photograph. They are pearlised, and I used a fine tapestry n to anchor a bead on the st at the apex of each knitweave triangle. Beg to bead once the armhole shaping is complete on back and front, and on the sleeve cap.

153

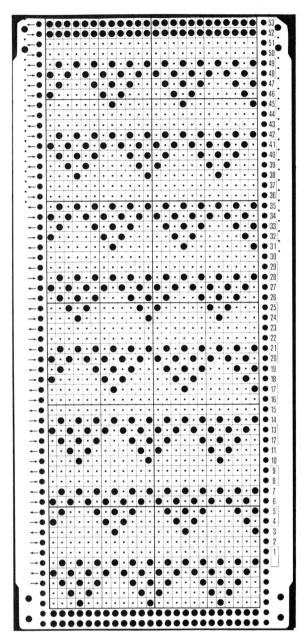

145 Card for Pattern 9. 8sts x 14rs

Back

Push 130ns into WP. Arrange for 1x1 rib. T1/1. K 24 rs. Transfer sts to MB. Arrange for patt. RC000. T6. Weave and k to RC112. Shape armholes. CO foll sts at beg of next 2rs and foll rs (2rs per number). 5, 3sts x 2, 2, 1 stitch (14 sts dec in 10rs). * Patt straight to RC82. Carr at left.

Shoulder

Cast off the foll sequences at beg of next and foll rs. 4sts x 4, 3. (19 sts dec in 20rs on each shoulder.) Note PC. At centre, take off 50sts onto WY. Tie and leave. Take back on WY and nylon cord sts at left. Cont on right. ** CO 4sts at beg of next r. K 1r. CO 3sts at beg of next r. Bring ns at left back into WP. Return PC. Lock and select. K to left. Beg at **.

Front

As back to *. Patt straight to RC44, Note PC. With WY, take off 32sts at centre neck. Tie and leave. Take back on WY and nylon cord sts at left. Proceed on right. K to left. ***. At centre neck CO foll sequences at beg of next and foll alt rs. 4, 3 x 2, 2 x 2, 1 stitch x 2 (16sts dec in 14rs). K straight to RC82. Carr at right.

Shoulder

CO the foll sequences at beg of next and foll alt rs. 4sts x 4, 3sts (19sts dec in 19rs). Carr at right. Pull back into WP ns at left. Arrange for patt. K 2rs. RC45. Follow back from ***, reading left for right.

Sleeve (2)

Push 98ns into WP. Cast on with WY. K 6rs. Carr at right. RC000. T6. Beg to patt k to RC42. Carr at right.

Armhole

RC000. CO foll sequences, 2rs per number at beg of next and foll rs. 4, 3, 2 x 2, 1 stitch x 4 (15sts dec at each side). RC16. K 2rs. CO 1 stitch at beg of next 2rs. Repeat 4rs x 11 altog. RC60. CO 1 stitch at beg of next 4rs, and then 2, 3, 4, 5sts (2rs per number). RC72. CO rem 14sts.

Cuffs (2)

Push 78ns into WP. With right side facing pick up 98sts, distributing extras evenly. Arrange for 1x1 rib. T1/1. K 12rs. T10/8. K 1r. Transfer to MB. Link-latch off.

Neckband

Push 170ns into WP. Arrange for 1x1 rib. RC000. T1/1. 3rs. T1/1.1. 3rs. T1.2/1.2. 3rs. T2/2. 3rs. RC12. Transfer to MB. St up left shoulder seam and, with wrong side facing, pick up sts round neck. Remove WY. T10. K 1r. Link-latch off.

Making up

St all seams. Insert sleeves, arranging gathers on top of shoulder. Give a light steam pat. Do not press.

Pattern 10: Man's medium-weight sweater

Size – 97cm
Measurements – as Fig. 147

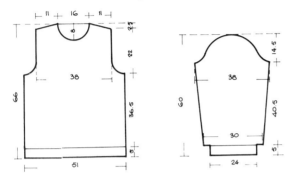

147 Measurements for man's medium-weight sweater (Pattern 10)

Materials – 225g Forsell's 2/16 wool (base), 245g DK wool (weft)
Pattern – as Fig. 148. Rolling repeat for 60rs. 24sts, 38rs. Card locked until top of yoke and sleeves for ORR pattern
Tension – 28sts, 44rs per 10cm. T5.1
Machine used – Knitmaster 700 plus weaving arm. SRP50 ribber
Notes – (1) I was going to turn the card upside down, but preferred it like this. The card was released 13.6cm below the top of the shoulder and sleeve. Mark on your charting device where you wish to re-introduce the rolling repeat.

(2) Notice how even fitted sleeves are becoming less fitted, and in menswear patterns, particularly from Japan, the sleeve is slightly gathered to the cuff for ease. This garment is a good sweater weight, and will, I hope, persuade knitters who have never yet attempted knitweave that it really is a knitting area they can no longer afford to neglect.

Back

Lock card on r1. Push 142ns into WP. Arrange for industrial rib (2 x 2, on H5). Using 2 ends of base and T3/4, k 24rs. Transfer to MB. Prepare

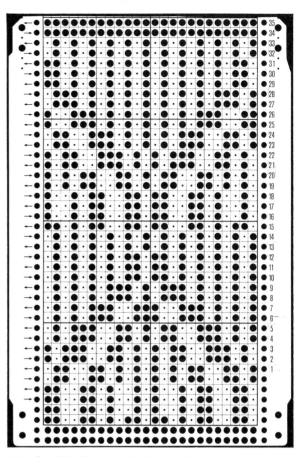

148 Card for Pattern 10. 24sts x 38rs

to knitweave. RC000. T5.1. Weave to r60. Lock card. Weave to r160. Shape armholes. RC000. CO foll sts at beg of next 2rs and foll rs, 2rs per number: 5, 4, 3, 2 x 2, 1 stitch x 2 (36sts in 14rs). Weave to RC36. Release card. * Weave to RC96.

Shoulder

CO foll sequences, 2rs per number, at beg of next and foll rs, 6sts x 5 (30sts cast off for shoulder in 10rs). Scrap off rem 46sts.

Front

As back to *. Weave to RC72. Shape neck. With a piece of spare WY, take off 24sts at centre. Tie and leave. Draw back on nylon cord sts at left. Note PC. Cont on right side. Weave to left. ** At beg of next and ev alt r on neck side, CO foll sequences: 4, 3, 2, 1 stitch x 2 (11sts CO in 9rs). Weave to RC96.

156

149 Pattern 10

Shoulder

CO 6sts x 5 on ev alt r. Left side, carr at right. Return PC. Pull sts into WP. Weave for 2rs. RC73. Cont from ** to end.

Sleeve (2)

With WY, cast on 84sts. Weave rolling repeat to r60. Lock card. At the same time inc 1 stitch at each end of 15th r x 8, 16th r x 3 (106sts). RC 168. Weave 6rs.

Armhole

RC000. Release card at r4. At same time CO foll sts at beg of next 2rs and foll rs, 2rs per number: 5, 4, 3, 2 (28sts dec in 8rs). Dec 1 stitch at beg of next 2rs. Repeat last 4rs x 7 altog. CO 1 stitch at beg of next 8rs. CO 2sts at beg of next 4rs and then 3, 4, 5, st sequences, 2rs per number. RC64. Cast off rem 14sts.

Cuffs

Carr at left. Push 70ns into WP. Pick up sts at base of sleeve, distributing extras evenly. Using 2 ends of base, T7, k to right. RC000. Arrange for 1 x 1 rib. T1/2. K 24rs. T10/10. K 1r. Transfer to MB. Link-latch off.

Neckband

Stitch up left shoulder seam. Carr at right. Push 146ns into WP. With right side facing, pick up sts round neck. T7. K 1r. Arrange for 1 x 1 rib. RC000. T3/4. K 4rs. T2.2/3.2. K 4rs. T2.1/3.1. K 4rs. T2/3. K 4rs. T5/6. K 1r (fold). Reverse. RC33. Transfer to MB. T7. K 2rs. Scrap off in 8rs WY.

Making up

St all seams. Back st neckband into place. Remove WY. Give light press.

Further reading

Books on knitweave

Chessum, Raymonde *Raymonde's Book of Weaving.* MSM publications, from Metropolitan Sewing Machines (see over)

Hansen, Rosemary *Easyweave: Machine Woven Garments* from PO Box 519, Robertson 6705, Cape Province, RSA

Palmer, Audrey *Create with Knitweave*

Palmer, Audrey *Create with Knitweave*, Supplement 1, from Palmer Publications, 152 Venice Road, Morningside, Durban 4001, RSA

Varvel, Pat *Knitweaving for Machine Knitters.* Varvel Designs, USA

Books containing sections on knitweave

Allen, John *The Machine Knitting Book* Dorling Kindersley, 1985

Davis, Joanna *Machine Knitting to suit your Mood* Pelham Books. 1982

Holborne, David *The Book of Machine Knitting* Batsford 1979

Kinder, Kathleen *A Resource Book Pattern Supplement* 1983. From Valley View, Station Road, Giggleswick, Settle, N. Yorkshire

Lewis and Weissman *A Machine Knitters' Guide to Creating Fabrics.* Lark, USA. 1986

Lorant, Tessa *The Batsford Book of Hand and Machine Knitting.* 1980

Palmer, Audrey *The Empisal Book of Linked Edgings and Finishings.* Empisal, RSA

Sharp, Sheila *Textured Patterns for Machine Knitting.* Batsford 1986

Weaver, Mary *Machine Knitting Technology* from 8, Craybrooke Road, Sidcup, Kent. DA4 9HJ

General reading

Harlow, Eve *The Art of Knitting* Collins

Hartley and Ingilby *The Old Handknitters of the Dales* Dalesman Books

Thomas, Mary *Knitting Book* Dover

Yarn suppliers

Index